Buying a Franchise

BUYING A FRANCHISE

BRIAN R. SMITH

and THOMAS L. WEST

THE STEPHEN GREENE PRESS • LEXINGTON, MASSACHUSETTS

First published in 1986 by The Stephen Greene Press, Inc.
Published simultaneously in Canada by Penguin Books Canada Limited
Distributed by Viking Penguin Inc., 40 West 23rd Street, New York, NY 10010.

The charts on pages 84-85, 87-88, and 90-95 are reprinted from Buying Your Own Small
Business by Brian R. Smith and Thomas L. West, published by The Stephen
Greene Press. Copyright © The Stephen Greene Press, Inc., 1985.

ISBN 0-8289-0573-X

CIP data available

Printed in the United States of America by
Hamilton Printing Company, Inc., Rensselaer, New York
Set in Times Roman
Designed by Victoria Hartman

To Dennis and Janette Smith.

B R S

To the kids, Patty, Jennifer, Sue, Jim, and Ron, who think it's neat to have an "author" for a father; to my colleague Brian Smith, who helped more than he knows; and to my wife, Barbara, for her never-ending support and patience.

T L W

Contents

Buying a Franchise

Introduction

If you have been considering going into business for yourself and feel, as millions do, that buying a franchise may be the thing to do, then this book is for you. Business publications and franchisors themselves will tell you that buying a franchise is a guarantee of success. We hear success rates of 95 percent to 99 percent being thrown around. The government seems to support these figures.

We're not sure where they get their statistics from, but we can't agree with them. The figures don't tell you about the franchisee in Des Moines who invested $100,000 in his business and then had to sell it to someone else for $15,000 because that was all he could get. The business is still operational, as the "statistics" indicate; the $85,000 loss, however, is not reflected anywhere.

Franchisors aren't very anxious to report failures within their system. Some buy back their failures. Others attempt to sell their distressed operations. A minority hope their failures will simply go away and still others carry a franchise on their records even though it's been closed for months. When a franchisor states they have 250 operating units, there may only be 200 actually open for business. Fifty have been closed and now are for sale.

Now, don't get the idea we think franchising is a poor way to get into business for yourself. We don't think that at all. Franchising is the safest form of independent business ownership, but we don't want you to think franchising is a sure thing for you. You can't give a franchisor some of your money and expect instant success. Consider franchising with the same clinical and critical eye you would any other investment.

Franchising is a very satisfactory way of starting your own business; it can be extremely rewarding, both personally and financially; it can free you of having to work for someone else. Are all franchises secure investments? Consider the following list:

- Chuck E Cheese Pizza Time Theater
- Mantle Men—Namath Girls
- Minnie Pearl's Chicken
- Jerry Lewis Theaters
- Arthur Treacher's Fish and Chips
- Lums
- Curry Copy Center
- Kentucky Roast Beef
- Chicken Delight

The entire list is long, that list of either total or near failures. It would be a fairly safe bet that millions of dollars were lost and thousands of dreams shattered.

Let's take one of these sad tales and see what happened.

Until 1979, Arthur Treacher's Fish and Chips was owned by Orange-co, Inc., of Lake Hamilton, Florida. Orange-co sold the business to a large

1

food company known primarily for its frozen fish cakes which were sold in supermarkets. We will omit the name of the company to protect the guilty.

The first mistake was made right off the bat. Arthur Treacher's had gained a reputation for quality fish. Franchisees used high-grade Atlantic cod. The frozen fish company substituted their tasteless, low-quality frozen fish cakes. Franchisees immediately voiced their objection to serving precooked, reheated, rubbery cakes in place of the valued cod. The new franchisor totally ignored their franchisees. It continued to collect fees, but provided no service. By late 1981, some 90% of the Arthur Treacher franchisees were refusing to pay royalties. Some were adding forbidden items to their line—crab legs, tacos, spaghetti. Many outlets either dropped the Arthur Treacher name or just went out of business.

In 2 years, the number of outlets had declined from 700 to 400. A court battle was in progress. Franchisees claimed the company impeded supplies (and poor supplies at that) and neglected its obligations.

The rest is history. If there are any Arthur Treacher locations left, we don't know of them.

Because of the problems unscrupulous franchisors were causing, the Federal Trade Commission (FTC), a part of the Department of Commerce of the U.S. government, enacted a "rule" which, in 1979, made franchisors disclose full information about their businesses. As we will see, the rule may have caused more problems for both franchisors and franchisees than it solved.

Unfortunately, many prospective franchisees believe the government actually approves the information from franchisors. It doesn't. For instance, here's the actual wording you'll find contained as a part of this disclosure material:

To protect you, we've required your franchisor to give you this information. *We haven't checked it, and don't know if it's correct.* It should help you make up your mind. Study it carefully. While it includes some information about your contract, don't rely on it alone to understand your contract. Read all of your contract carefully. Buying a franchise is a complicated investment. Take your time to decide. If possible show your contract to an advisor, like a lawyer or an accountant. If you find anything you think may be wrong or anything important that's been left out, you should let us know about it. It may be against the law.

There may also be laws on franchising in your state. Ask your state agencies about them.

Federal Trade Commission
Washington, DC 20580

Despite that wording, many people still feel the government is somehow involved. Because of the seemingly implied assurance, despite the wording, prospective franchisees may believe the government has passed judgment—a positive judgment. It hasn't.

All this legislation may actually work against you. For one thing, it adds to the franchisor's costs—legal interpretation, paperwork, accounting charges. Imagine who pays this added expense? Also, as we'll cover later, the FTC regulation indirectly fixes prices: prices you'll pay for that franchise. It also limits your ability to negotiate a better deal for yourself.

So, the same law that is designed to protect you can also work to your disadvantage.

Despite what we've just said, we still believe that franchising offers one viable alternative to getting into your own businees. In this book we want to dispel the myths and focus on reality.

Be aware, then, of the two "Myths of Franchising":

1. Franchising is a sure thing.
2. The government protects you.

Now let's look at the reality of franchising.

Successes and Failures

In this book about how to get started in a franchised business we cover franchising, successes and failures, the franchising market, some self-assessment procedures, how to select and analyze franchise opportunities, legal and ethical considerations—what you can expect an honest franchisor to do for you and what is expected of you—and, finally, some material on the early operational stages.

There are three things this book is *not:*

1. It's not a book about how to start your own business. If you prefer that route, we suggest *Raising Seed Money For Your Own Business* by Brian R. Smith (1984, The Stephen Greene Press) as a more appropriate text.
2. This isn't a book about how to buy a business, including an existing, established franchise. For that alternative, see our guide, *Buying Your Own Small Business* (1985, The Stephen Greene Press).
3. It won't tell you how to run your franchise after you open the doors. If you're working with a successful franchisor, the company will give you the proper initial training. If you want more information, see *How to Prosper In Your Own Business* (Brian R. Smith, 1980, The Stephen Greene Press).

Now let's begin by defining the terms we'll be using most frequently:

Franchise: In its purest sense, a franchise is a legal agreement. If I come up with a new way of washing windows, and I let you use my name, special soap, tools, and methods of running such a business, if you pay me for that opportunity and operate the way I tell you, our agreement to that effect is called a franchise. It's your business, but I control what you do. Many people look at a McDonald's restaurant and say, "That's a franchise." That's only partially correct: the land and building aren't the franchise, they are only visible signs of what's contained in the franchise agreement. When we speak of "buying a franchise" we really mean buying the agreement itself, which may contain clauses about supplies, equipment, and even real estate which then become part of the entire package.

Franchisor: For legal and accounting reasons, this is usually a corporation. As a legal entity, the franchisor owns the patents, trademarks, methods, and supplies that it allows others to use under their own auspices. For example, specific McDonald's menu, methods and procedures, and only these, are found exclusively in their establishments. Each owner of a McDonald's accepts this as part of his or her business agreement with that franchisor. A franchisor differs from a corporation operating a chain of stores because the managers of the latter are company employees, not self-employed business people.

Franchisee: Normally this is you, the person who owns the franchise. Although you may form your own corporation and even have investors, when we use the term in the pages ahead, put yourself in that position.

Although this book covers franchising in general, it's not intended for individuals considering a large, expensive, well-established franchise like McDonald's, because the purchase of such a franchise is *big* business. How big? If you wanted a McDonald's, for example, you might need over $1 million and have to wait a year or more.

This book focuses on franchises other than McDonald's for a very special reason. Most books are aimed at those interested in acquiring a large franchise. However, the majority of franchisees in the United States and other countries own relatively small businesses, those grossing less than $300,000 annually; and the majority of those interested in acquiring a franchise don't have a million or two in the bank.

There's another reason for our choosing this route. We've all heard success stories of franchisees owning and operating one of the large franchises—owner's salaries in the hundreds of thousands of dollars, no chance of failure, vacations in Aruba. This has led to a belief that franchising guarantees success, regardless of the type of business; that simply isn't true. There have been franchising schemes set up to hoodwink honest people out of their money with little or no intent of ever getting the business off the ground. There have been failures of franchisors once they were established, not through unethical behavior so much as stupidity or greed.

We want to give you as much good guidance as possible. We want to show franchising as it is, neither a guaranteed way to become a millionaire nor a hideous scam.

With all this in mind, let's begin our journey by looking at some franchising failures and success stories.

Mary Knolls was a high-school English teacher who had one dream after her retirement—to be in her own business: no boss, no fixed schedule, no arbitrary rules and regulations. For ten years she saved diligently and at age 62 left teaching with a small pension, another few hundred dollars a month from Social Security, and $20,000 in savings. Although she wanted to be self-employed, she decided against starting a business

or buying an existing one because her business experience was limited. Among the many articles she read in the popular press and magazines for retired persons were several touting the franchise route as the easiest and safest for people like her. Good franchisors, said the articles, provided the necessary training and showed franchisees how to operate their own business and make a good living from them.

Her reading convinced Mary that buying a franchise was the best approach for her, but what franchise should she invest her hard-earned dollars in?

Mary had always been interested in plants and flowers, having the proverbial "green thumb," and so when she spotted the following advertisement, it aroused her interest immediately:

BE IN YOUR OWN BUSINESS!! Become independent and wealthy in the horticulture business. Proven method supplies small plants and seeds to retail establishments, assures high earnings with a minimum of effort. Only a limited number of franchises available, so act now! Fill out the coupon below and we'll send you information showing this easy path to success. ACT NOW! Your future is in your hands.

Mary mailed the coupon and received a slick package of promotional material describing a franchise that provided modular display stands, plants, seedlings, and seeds the franchisee placed in supermarkets. The franchisee paid the grocers a fixed rental to leave the display in their stores, and then re-stocked the shelves as eager patrons snapped up the horticultural bargains. The literature also included exciting statistics about the phenomenal growth in the sale of houseplants.

Mary had only had the information for two days when she received a phone call from Ralph Johnson, the regional manager for Plants-For-Everyone. He said he was only in town for two days and asked if he could come by for an informal chat to answer any questions Mary might have. She agreed and Ralph was at her apartment in half an hour.

However, rather than the "informal chat" he promised, Ralph launched into a high-pressure sales presentation. Although the company had a number of different plans available as part of a limited time offer, he suggested Mary become a "four-star dealer" because there were 22 supermarkets within ten miles of her home. His very convincing statistics showed how, as a four-star dealer, she could earn $1,200 per store per year. Simple mulitiplication told her she could net $26,400 annually from the stores in her neighborhood—almost twice her teaching salary.

All Mary had to do was part with $25,000 ("Why, Mary, that's less than what you'll make in your first year," said the enthusiastic Mr. Johnson) to cover the franchise fee of $3,500, her training, the modular racks, and supplies. Ralph assured her that her income would begin coming in immediately, once the plant stands were in the stores.

"But," Mary said, "I only have $20,000 in the bank."

Mr. Johnson's eyes widened sympathetically and he flashed two rows of pearly teeth. "That's no problem, Mary. We can finance the additional $5,000 and you can pay us back from your profits. I want you to be able to take advantage of this offer before it runs out in another week. Because of our tremendous success, our fees will be increasing by 10 percent. We'd hate to lose you as part of our team."

Ralph left Mary with a contract (which he signed), some more slick literature, and a promissory note (which he also signed) for $5,000 at 24.6 percent interest.

The next day Mary received a call from Mr. Rottoni, Ralph Johnson's supervisor. He said how impressed Ralph was with her, and how important it was that she mail in her $20,000 check and all the paperwork to beat the impending fee increase. Mr. Rottoni said how anxious Plants-For-Everyone was to have such a qualified person as Mary Knolls as one of their family of successful franchisors.

Mary withdrew all her savings, signed the documents, and mailed it all to a post office box in Denver. In a week she received her "training material"—ten photocopied pages of information about how to convince supermarket managers to put Plants-For-Everyone "islands" in their stores. Two days later a truck delivered 30 cardboard boxes containing a collection of orange plastic shelving parts with instructions for their assembly, plastic flowerpots, some envelopes of seeds, and some potting soil.

As she opened box after box in her modest apartment, Mary was shocked. There were no plants; she had to grow the seeds herself before she could get into business. Undaunted, she rearranged furniture, placing tables, desks, and other flat-surfaced furnishings by her few windows. These were then covered with her collection of plastic flowerpots, each filled with potting soil and seeds. Mary's own knowledge of gardening told her that her apartment fell far short of supplying the optimum growing conditions, but it was the best she could do.

After stacking the remaining boxes in one corner of the living room, she put together her first "island" from the components supplied; it was garish and rickety at best. Feeling a bit uneasy about her investment, she decided to concentrate her efforts on securing supermarket customers instead.

After driving around and visiting the managers of the 22 stores for six weeks, Mary discovered the following:

- Fifteen of the stores were chain operations and the managers could do nothing without the approval of the parent company. All doubted their superiors would permit independent operations within their stores—that used up valuable and precisely calculated floor space.
- Five stores already had plant and flower sections.
- One store was about to close.
- One store manager said he might be interested but wanted twice as much to rent Mary the space as Plants-For-Everyone proposed.

In the meantime Mary received a letter from a nationwide finance company notifying her of their purchase of her $5,000 note from Plants-For-Everyone. They added a 1 percent "service fee."

Mary wrote to the Plants-For-Everyone headquarters: no response. She called the toll-free number and was informed by a computerized voice that the telephone had been disconnected. After some research in the library, she came across an article in an obscure Colorado newspaper detailing the demise of the plant franchise operation. Messrs. Johnson, Rottoni, and six others had dropped from sight after pocketing over half a million dollars. Mary was left with a few unsaleable supplies, an empty bank account, and a note for $5,000 plus interest and service fees.

Quite a story, isn't it? Is it unique? No. Thousands of people have been bilked in the same way. What did Mary do wrong? Re-read the story and see if you can spot her errors. Later we'll cover the necessary steps to prevent you from becoming another Mary Knolls.

To be sure, franchising is hardly a nationwide scam. There are now over 2,000 franchisors (companies) with over half a million stores and operations. Most of them are successful; some are not. Obviously Mary Knolls ran into an unethical group of individuals and succumbed because of her own ignorance. We don't want that to happen to you.

We've looked at a failure; now let's look at a success. An article in the January 7, 1985 issue of *Newsweek* entitled "The McDonald's of Teaching" detailed the rapid growth of a company called Sylvan Learning Corporation. The company was founded by W. Berry Fowler, himself a secondary-school teacher and part-time entrepreneur. As is true with all those who start successful businesses, Mr. Fowler found a need and satisfied it. In 1980 he opened an instruction center in Portland, Oregon for students who wanted tutorial help. Now he's president and principal stockholder of a $5 million company which has sold nearly 150 franchises for Sylvan Learning Centers.

It costs a franchisee from $65,000 to $85,000 to obtain the franchise (the fee is $27,500) and acquire an advertising campaign, teaching materials, supplies, and furniture. As with any business, earnings of the franchisee (often a former teacher) vary depending on personal efforts; but the *Newsweek* article cited one Sylvan owner in greater Boston who plans to open two more centers *each* of which could produce before-tax profits of $100,000.

When most people see the word "franchise" they immediately think of McDonald's, Kentucky Fried Chicken, Dunkin' Donuts, or Burger King. Those with a bit more business experience might also recognize franchises such as Midas (mufflers and shocks), General Business Services (accounting and consulting services for small businesses), or Dunhill (personnel placement). Yet, how many of us would have been visionary enough to think of a "franchised school"?

Let's look at another area of franchising that may surprise you, that of veterinary medicine. First we'll look at a failure and then a success.

The failure was a company called National Pet Care Centers (NPCC) whose basic concept was sound. Individual veterinary practices became NPCC's by paying a franchise fee that assured the practice owners "professionally developed and administered marketing programs," "better business systems," and "group advertising"—all of which would result in an "ever-increasing client base." The concept of "overlaying" a franchise on an existing business has been well proven, especially in the real estate industry, with national franchising firms such as ERA and Century 21.

The demise of NPCC was detailed in an article by Christoper J. Fiorello, "Are Franchised Hospitals Worth All That Money?" (*Veterinary Economics,* June 1984, pp. 54–61). Here are some of the critical points noted in that article:

1. NPCC's two owners claimed to have a board of directors consisting of a number of financial executives when, in fact, the board consisted of only the owners.
2. Potential franchisees were shown storyboards for TV commercials supposedly prepared by a nationally known advertising agency. Apparently no ads were ever broadcast.
3. NPCC executives violated Federal Trade Commission regulations in several areas, the most significant of which was charging different initial joining fees.
4. One of the investors noted that, to his knowledge, NPCC did not pay its 1983 federal withholding tax to the IRS.
5. A veterinarian in California bought an NPCC franchise in 1983 that included a mailing in her name of 10,000 brochures telling cat owners about the importance of feline rabies immunization. She received *one* inquiry from this "professionally developed and administered marketing program," and later discovered approximately 5,000 of the recipients didn't even own cats!
6. NPCC executives wrote checks for thousands of dollars to a consulting firm which was, in fact, the two top executives themselves.

The failure of NPCC was much like the failure of Plants-For-Everyone—fraudulent and unethical behavior on the part of the franchisor coupled with a lack of pre-purchase analysis and research on the part of the franchisee.

On the heels of the demise of NPCC comes VETCARE℠ Animal Hospitals founded by Steven L. Meier, DVM, and Holly F. Meier. Steve is a veterinarian who operated a successful practice in Connecticut for a number of years and Holly has a background in business, as well as graphic arts. Rather than the conversion system offered by NPCC, VETCARE offers an entire practice, set up and ready to run—including the building, fully equipped and stocked with the necessary drugs and supplies. The franchisees, who are normally younger veterinarians with several years of practice under their belts, are given:

- A professional advertising campaign.
- A client and public relations program.
- Practice management training and consultation.
- Accounting services.
- Financial analysis.
- The financial benefits of a large-volume group drugs and supply purchase.
- Access to business advisors.
- A small-business computer and the necessary software to maintain the practice.

It's reasonable to assume solid franchisors give rise to solid businesses, but is it possible to have problems with an ethical franchise? Let's consider the case of Pizza Time Theatre (PTT). (See "A Noisy Decline" by Stephen Traub, *Financial World,* November 30, 1983, pp. 40–43.)

PTT was the brainchild of someone who had already proven himself one of the most brilliant and creative entrepreneurs to come along—Nolan Bushnell, the inventor of "Pong" and a founder of Atari. When Atari was sold to Warner Communications for $28 million, Bushnell took the PTT concept with him. PTT was a pizza restaurant with a video arcade in one room and computer-controlled, singing robots in others. From 1980 to 1983 the number of PTTs went from seven to over 200 with annual sales topping $100 million. Then the problems began.

Three factors contributed to the failure of several locations:

1. Customers considered the $30 a typical family of four would spend in a single visit too high.
2. Many considered both the food and the service inferior.
3. The arcade business declined.

The year 1984 was to see PTT go into a tailspin. Bushnell resigned early in the year after it was announced that the company lost $81 million in 1983 with $75 million of that occurring in the last 16 weeks of the year. The company got themselves a new president who resigned after four months. They were sued by Prudential, one of their investors. The Bank of California notified PTT in March that they were in default on the loan. It was also in March that they filed for protection under Chapter 11 of the federal bankruptcy laws; debts were shown to be in excess of $100 million.

Finally in September, Brock Hotel Corporation agreed to acquire 60 PTT restaurants to merge with its Show Biz Pizza Place.

We might also speculate that the concept of the business was confusing. Is PTT a pizza parlor, a game center, or some kind of electronic puppet show? A mixed message is a very difficult thing to sell to the public. (One of us had three uncles who opened an establishment that sold gasoline, liquor, and parakeets! When the business failed they had enough gas to fill their own tanks and a dozen alcoholic budgies.)

What happens to the franchisee if the franchisor runs into difficulties? If the franchisor stumbles, or even fails, in business, does this mean the franchisees are similarly doomed? An article in the April 25, 1983 issue of *Forbes* magazine ("When Love Is Gone" by Barbara Rudolph, p. 114) describes what happened to one franchisor, Quickprint, Inc. Quickprint had 525 instant-printing stores which operated under the name of Big Red Q Quickprint. Some 49 franchisees brought suit against the franchisor claiming:

1. The company received kickbacks from suppliers of the printing equipment franchisees were required to buy.
2. Quickprint failed to give the owners the marketing and sales assistance promised.
3. The chief executive of Quickprint spent too much time hustling new franchisees.
4. The company essentially abandoned them.

It's not surprising to read in the *Forbes* article that a number of franchisees were withholding royalty payments.

While we're talking about the printing business, let's examine a case where the collapse of a franchisor may have actually benefitted the franchisees. Curry Copy Centers of America, Inc., went out of business in 1978, leaving over 200 operating stores, most of them highly successful. How could such a thing happen? The story we get (and it's not documented) is that Curry may have been *too* helpful. Apparently Curry began properly; they ran a pilot store in Worcester, Massachusetts, for two years, and when it succeeded, franchises were sold. However, because of a misunderstanding, some franchisees believed all they had to do was to hang out a Curry sign and customers would flock to their doors. As with most businesses, this doesn't happen; there must be a marketing effort—sales calls, advertising, mailings. The franchisees turned to Curry for help and Curry quickly responded by sending teams of their own people into the stores. The financial burden of maintaining these teams plus a too-rapid expansion caused the downfall.

What was the net effect of Curry's failure on its franchisees? Most franchisees continued in business and saw a dramatic increase in profits because they no longer had to pay the 5 percent royalty on gross sales. Why do we say dramatic? Let's take a store grossing $200,000 annually, earning the owner a 5 percent (or $10,000) profit after tax and royalty payment. When the franchisor failed, the 5 percent or $10,000 previously paid to them as royalties became part of the franchisee's profit—increasing it from $10,000 to $20,000, a 100 percent increase!

In talking with one very savvy owner of a Curry Copy Center (he still uses the name) we learned he was smart enough to have a special clause written into his franchise agreement. The clause stipulated that if Curry itself failed, the relationship between him and the franchisor would cease once and for all time. Although it never became an issue, without that clause he would have been liable for royalties if Curry had chosen to sell their business.

And, finally, let's examine another documented story with a fascinating twist. Can a franchisee's phenomenal success create ill-will between him or her and the franchisor? Consider the case of Everett G. Attebury, who owns 77 Jitney-Jungle convenience stores. (For further details see an article titled "One Jobber's Franchise Experience: 'Wish to Hell I Never Heard of Them' " in the November 1982 issue of *National Petroleum News.*) Attebury began his franchising career by opening a single Jr. Food Mart with a $30,000 investment. The store did about twice as much business as he expected and he increased his number of outlets. However, in 1980 he also opened his own chain of stores called Crown Food Mart, a violation of his contract with Jitney, who therefore took him to court. They won and now Attebury pays franchise fees on all stores, his own included, which amounted to $150,000 in 1982. Mr. Attebury's comments in the *NPN* article are indeed stinging. He is quoted as saying, "Do not sign a franchise. Why? They (the franchisor) have got an oil well. In my case they got fees for 15 years for about six months' work that was done over four years ago."

Well, we could certainly argue both sides of the issue. It's easy to see Mr. Attebury's point, but we can also sympathize with the franchisor because Attebury's success (he made $600,000 in 1980) *is* dependent to one degree or another on Jitney-Jungle.

Now that we've looked at franchise successes and failures, let's put things in perspective. There are three ways to own your own business: start one, buy an already operating one, or buy a franchise. Although absolute statistics are nearly impossible to come by, here's a summary of the probablities of success for the three approaches:

Starting a business: For every ten businesses started from scratch, only two survive beyond five years—a 20 percent chance for survival.

Buying a business: For every ten businesses purchased, at least six make it and maybe as many as eight—an average of a 70 percent success rate.

Buying a franchise: The best figures available suggest a 90 percent success rate. This may be high.

If these numbers are correct, your chances of making it in your own business are 1.3 times better if you choose franchising over buying a business, and a whopping 4.5 times better than when starting your own. There are, of course, advantages and disadvantages to each route, especially when you consider your own makeup and personal desires, two critical areas we'll be discussing later.

The point we've been trying to make isn't to focus on failure but merely to increase your awareness that it does happen in franchising. If you're careful and you follow the course we suggest, you'll raise the probability of success. And that's what we want for you.

Does a franchise sound like the best route for you? In the next chapter we'll study the concept of franchising in detail—where it came from, where it's going, and what it means to you as a potential franchisee.

CHAPTER 2

Franchising: An Overview

HOW LARGE IS FRANCHISING?

To answer this question, let's look at the following table:

	1970	1980	1984
Number of Franchised Operations	396,000	442,400	461,700
Total Sales of These Operations (billions $)	117	336	457
Sales of All Retail Trade (billions $)	368	963	1267
U.S. Gross National Product (GNP) (billions $)	993	2632	3665

The terms are self-explanatory, but in case you have forgotten, the GNP is the total annual value of every dollar spent in the United States by consumers, industry, and government. We suspect this is determined by a "GNP Machine" in Washington that inches up every time you buy a candy bar, IBM sells a computer, or the Defense Department purchases a bomber.

Let's see what happened to franchise sales versus both retail sales and the GNP in the 15 years covered by our table:

	1970	1980	1984
Franchise Sales to Retail Sales (%)	32	35	36
Franchise Sales to GNP (%)	12	13	12

Franchising as a percent of all the goods and services sold in the United States remained relatively constant, but grew as a percent of retail trade. These figures indicate the franchising industry is huge, but let's dissect the 1984 total sales value and see how accurate the U.S. Department of Commerce's derivation really is. In the first place, this value includes the sales of company-owned establishments, those managed and operated by company employees rather than a self-employed franchised owner. By definition these aren't franchises at all and the $63 billion (or 13.8%) they contribute to the $457-billion figure is misleading. Secondly, we must look at two very large groups contributing to the total which aren't really true franchises either: gasoline service stations (19.1%) and automobile/truck dealers (a whopping 45.7%). These businesses charge no franchise or royalty fee and are only elaborate forms of authorized dealerships. If we add our three categories together, we find we must exclude almost four-fifths (actually 78.6%) of the total reported sales of franchised operations.

What's included in the remaining 21.4 percent? Here's a tally:

Kind of Business	Percent of 1984 Reported Sales
Fast Food Restaurants	6.3
Soft Drink Bottlers	3.4
Non-food Retailing	2.3
Hotels/Motels/Campgrounds	2.1
Business Aids/Services*	1.7
Automotive Products/Services	1.5
Food Retailing	1.5
Convenience Stores	1.0
Auto/Truck Rental	0.4
Construction/Maintenance	0.4
Other	0.8
	21.4

*includes tax preparation, employment agencies, printing and copying, accounting, general and miscellaneous business services.

Included in the "Other" category are franchises involved in education, laundry and dry cleaning, recreation and travel, equipment rental, and a few other businesses which are not listed by type but called simply "miscellaneous" by the government.

So now we know the figures are "loaded," and when someone says franchising produces one-eighth of our GNP, the real figure is more like *one-fortieth!*

Before we leave this number-crunching, let's take a look at what kinds of franchised businesses grew and which did not. From 1982 to 1984, four groups grew more than 25 percent in terms of the number of franchisee-owned establishments:

Kind of Business	Percent Growth, 1982–1984
Educational Services	75
Printing and Copying	40
Auto/Truck Rental	36
Equipment Rental	27

Other categories such as automotive products/services, tax preparation services, hotels/motels/campgrounds, and non-food retailing had growth rates less than 4 percent in those two years.

Interestingly, three categories showed an actual decline: auto/truck dealers, gasoline service stations, and soft drink bottlers. Because the first two aren't true franchises and the third requires a sizeable investment beyond a single business owner's capacity, we won't be concerning ourselves with these in this book.

HOW DID FRANCHISING BEGIN?

In 1886, an enterprising druggist by the name of John S. Pemberton stirred up an interesting drink containing sugar, molasses, spices, and a now-illegal drug—cocaine. You guessed it; it's what we now know as Coca-Cola (although it no longer contains what a few have dubbed the "queen of drugs"), and only those licensed by Pemberton were permitted to manufacture and bottle it. Shortly thereafter, in 1902, another druggist, Louis K. Liggett, offered his colleagues the right to use his successful business name, and Rexall drugstores became a familiar sight across America.

As industry grew rapidly in the early years of this century, franchising expanded into other areas. We became fascinated with the automobile, and automobile manufacturers and oil companies began franchising independent business owners. Soon franchising was available in almost any type of business imaginable: soft ice cream, coin-operated laundries, home cleaning services, and farm equipment dealers.

The greatest franchising story of them all, however, is that of a young salesman named Ray Kroc. Among the products Ray sold to soda fountains and small restaurants was a machine which could simultaneously prepare six milkshakes. When the owners of a California restaurant ordered eight of these machines, inquisitive Kroc simply had to find out why. Before delivering the equipment, he parked outside this restaurant with its red-and-white squares and rather silly-looking painted yellow arch. After two days' observation he knew the arch wasn't painted yellow: it was gold. Real gold! He made an offer the two owners from Bedford, New Hampshire, couldn't refuse: several million dollars—not for their restaurant but for the perpetual, worldwide rights to their name and their basic restauranting approach. The brothers McDonald accepted the offer, and the rest is franchising history. Franchised restaurants weren't new; White Tower, Nathan's and the (then) famous Joe & Nemo's all preceded McDonald's. However, Ray Kroc offered a complete turnkey system with his restaurant franchises, and that was new.

Around the same time, a gentle man of 65, Harlan Sanders, took a completely different route. He drove around the country convincing people they could enjoy life and make money selling chicken. As our country was shortening its borders as a result of air travel and interstate highways, "Colonel" Sanders was peddling "shortening" of a different kind—his famous herb and spice recipe and a way of cooking chicken that he called Kentucky Fried Chicken.

WHERE IS FRANCHISING NOW?

Think of any industry: There's probably at least one franchise operating within it. There are franchises to clean toilets, mow lawns, teach kids, feed us, give personal financial counseling, and cut hair. The following list of business categories and examples will give you an idea of how far franchising has come:

Categories	Example(s)
Automotive Products/ Services	AAMCO Transmissions, Inc.
	Ziebart Rustproofing Co.
Auto/Trailer Rentals	Avis Rent-A-Car System Inc.
Beauty Salons/Supplies	Edie Adams Cut & Curl
Business Aids/Services	General Business Services, Inc.
	Muzak
	VR Business Brokers, Inc.
Campgrounds	Kampgrounds of America, Inc.
Children's Products	Baby-Tenda Corp.
Clothing and Shoes	Knapp Shoe Co.
Construction/Remodeling	Energy Doctor, Inc.
	New England Log Homes, Inc.
Cosmetics/Toiletries	Boyd's Madison Avenue
Dental Centers	Dentcare Systems, Ltd.
Drug Stores	Dependon Rx

Categories	Example(s)
Educational Products/ Services	Evelyn Wood Reading Dynamics, Inc.
	Mind Power, Inc.
Employment Services	Dunhill Personnel System, Inc.
Equipment Rental	Taylor Rental Corp.
Foods—Donuts	Mister Donut of America, Inc.
Foods—Grocery	Quick Stop Markets, Inc.
Foods—Ice Cream	Baskin Robbins, Inc.
Foods—Pancakes	International House of Pancakes
Foods—Restaurants	McDonald's Corp.
Health Services	Gloria Stevens Figure Salons
	Nursefinders
Hearing Aids	RCI, Inc.
Home Furnishings/Services	Kleen Brite Systems
	Siesta Sleep Shop, Inc.
Insurance	Pridemark Corp.
Laundries & Dry Cleaning	Martin Franchises, Inc.
Lawn and Garden	Lawn King, Inc.
Maintenance and Cleaning	Mr. Rooter Corp.
Motels and Hotels	Sheraton Inns, Inc.
Optical Products/Services	Pearle Vision Centers
Paint and Decorating	Davis Paint Co.
Pet Shops	Docktor Pet Centers, Inc.
Printing	PIP-Postal Instant Press
Real Estate	Century 21 Real Estate Corp.
Recreation and Travel	Go-Kart Track Systems
	Travel Travel Inc.
Retailing (Other)	Computerland Corp.
	Heritage Clock Co.
	Little Professor Book Centers, Inc.
	Radio Shack
Security Systems	Dictograph Security Systems
Swimming Pools	California Pools, Inc.
Tools	Mac Tools, Inc.
Vending	Canteen Corp.
Water Conditioning	Culligan International Co.
Wholesale	Machinery Wholesalers Corp.

And this is only a partial listing!

WHAT EXACTLY IS FRANCHISING?

First, let's start with what it isn't. Any kind of simple resale arrangement isn't a franchise. If you think this book is the greatest thing you've ever read and want to sell it to others, you contact the publisher and they agree to sell you a certain quantity of books at a discount. No franchise is created. A simple distributorship isn't a franchise either, even though you may have a protected territory and training—two things you can also expect from an established franchisor. We have some types of business arrangements, such as True Value Hardware, which come very close to franchising in terms of the services they provide. However, True Value is essentially a retailing cooperative; they don't charge a franchise fee.

Another scheme which some confuse with franchising is what's known as pyramiding, and it's illegal in most states. The simplest example of pyramiding is the chain letter containing a list of five names. You send a dollar to the person whose name appears at the top of the list, remove his or her name, and add your own to the bottom. You then send copies of the letter with its new list to ten friends. The reason why the scheme is appealing is the same reason which defeats it: simple mathematics. If for every round the letter makes, the number of participants increases tenfold, it takes 5 rounds to get you to the top of the list, and then, theoretically, you should receive $100,000 (10 times itself 5 times). However, if we need 100,000 participants to generate the case for the fifth person on the list, after ten rounds the number of participants must be 10,000,000,000—more than twice the world's population! In other words, only those in the very top tiers of the pyramid make out because there simply aren't enough people to sustain the system at lower levels.

Unfortunately in business one kind of pyramiding is legal. In these schemes you purchase a dealership in something like housewares and then you can sell dealerships to others. Obviously dealers who buy their dealerships from other dealers are further down in the pyramid and their likelihood of success decreases accordingly. Fortunately, such quasi-ethical arrangements are usually not true franchises.

What, then, *is* a true franchise? In its most basic form it's a legal contract, an agreement between two entities, the franchisor (most often a corporation) and the franchisee (usually a single person). Being a contract, it must meet the five criteria of any contract:

1. There must be an offer. If I want to sell my car to you, I must make a clear offer to do so—put an ad in the paper, tape a sign to its window, mention it to you at work.
2. There must be an acceptance. You must agree to buy my car and this acceptance doesn't have to be in writing. One court held that a nod of the head was sufficient to be deemed an acceptance.
3. There must be consideration. Our legal system recognizes two kinds of consideration: valuable consideration which is usually money, and good consideration which is a feeling. (Remember the old "alienation of affection"?)
4. The parties must be competent. This criterion rules out minors, alcoholics, the mentally ill.
5. The contract must be for a legal purpose: a written agreement that sets up a pyramiding scam isn't legal and therefore not a contract.

Now let's turn our attention to franchising specifically. There are a few essential elements to any franchise agreement:

- First, the franchisor must own or possess the rights to something—a name, method, business format, proprietary process, patent, copyright, trademark, goods, equipment, reputation—that the franchisor is willing to license to someone else.
- Second, the franchisor must indeed license others to use its rights. This it does by accepting the franchisee's payment of fees—normally a one-time franchisee fee as well as a continuing fee called a royalty.
- Third, the franchisor must be willing to execute a contract spelling out the rights and duties of both franchisor and franchisee.

Above and beyond these three "necessary and sufficient conditions" (to borrow a legal phrase), there are other common elements in a franchise agreement with a well-established, ethical franchisor:

1. The franchisor provides training.
2. The franchisor maintains a constant and continuing relationship with its franchisees, realizing it

(the franchisor) can't succeed unless its franchisees succeed.

3. The franchisor accepts that the franchisee makes an investment in the business *and* owns the business.

4. The franchisee, over and beyond paying an initial fee and a continuing royalty, may be required to buy supplies and services exclusively from the franchisor or its approved suppliers.

5. The franchisee must agree to operate his or her business in accord with the rules and guidelines established by the franchisor.

6. The franchisee is given a territory, but it may not be protected.

FROM THE FRANCHISOR'S STANDPOINT

Let's look at why franchisors do what they do and how their actions can affect the franchisee. First, let's look at the franchisor's advantages of franchising:

1. The biggest advantage is the ability to expand rapidly without needing the large amounts of capital necessary to form a comparable chain-store operation.

   Authors Phillip White and Albert Bates, writing in the copyrighted February 17, 1984 issue of *Marketing News* ("Franchising will remain retailing fixture, but its salad days have long since gone"), compared the growth of Wendy's, a franchised fast-food operation, to The Gap, which operates company-owned stores selling clothes to young adults. In 1970 both firms had two units, but by the end of 1983, The Gap had 587 outlets compared to Wendy's 2,716.

2. Since each store is independently owned, the franchisors deal with a more motivated group than if these same people were branch managers. Because each franchisee accepts more responsibility for his or her own operation, the franchisor experiences less staff problems than those involved in the day-to-day management of chains.

3. The nature of securing growth capital for franchise expansion is quite different from funding comparable expansion in company-owned outlets. Usually when a corporation expands, it must either sell ownership which creates stockholders (owners) or borrow money that must be paid back with interest.

There are also disadvantages and possible pitfalls for the franchisor.

1. In general, company-owned stores are more profitable to the owning company and they are easier to control.

2. The franchisor's investment in franchisee training is substantial.

3. Franchisors must consistently enforce their standards of quality. They must be ever-alert to changes and therefore must maintain a continuing research and development program.

4. Probably the area having the greatest problem-creating potential is the franchisees themselves. How does a franchisor pick a franchisee? The sleazier ones use one criteria—money. The better ones go into the individual's background interests. Franchisors want franchisees to succeed, but they want them to succeed as *their* franchisees. Here are some typical concerns franchisors have about franchisees:

   a. The franchisee could get ideas about being independent; the franchisor may be training and setting up a future competitor.

   b. Independent business people are just that—independent. It may be difficult to get franchisees to make changes (such as building renovation) especially if things are going well.

   c. There probably isn't a franchisee on this earth who hasn't at least thought about hiding income to reduce royalty payments.

FROM THE FRANCHISEE'S STANDPOINT

The main advantages of franchising for the franchisee center around the franchising's reduced risk. The franchisee's personal investment is normally less than it would be to start or buy a comparable business. Also, if a potential franchisee has to secure outside financing, such as a commercial bank loan, the bank is more comfortable with the franchise, assuming the franchise has established itself and is not a new and untried concept.

As we might suspect, a major advantage for the franchisee is the many benefits resulting from the relationship with the franchisor. The franchisee can expect:

• Training.
• The use of a recognized name and image.

- National advertising.
- A *proven* method of doing business.
- Cost-saving, bulk purchase capability.
- Management consulting and assistance.
- New products and services.
- A protected territory.

Not every franchisor provides everything on our list, but most of the better ones do.

How about the minus side of the register for the franchisee? The primary disadvantage is rooted in the issue of control. Obviously if you open your own business, you can do what you want—pick the name, sell your products and services, choose your location, buy things where and when you choose. Some folks simply don't want someone else to tell them how to run their own business, regardless of how sound the other's approach may be. If you're that kind of person, stay far away from franchising. Do it on your own and your own way.

How extensive are these restrictions and limitations? The next time you walk into any nationally established, fast-food restaurant, look around. The decor is specified; employees wear prescribed uniforms, even the napkins must be a certain size. One franchisor's policy manual even specifies when you empty the trash cans. There are also restrictions governing the sale of the business; under most franchise arrangements, the buyer must be approved by the franchisor.

Other disadvantages include:

- The payment of fees and royalties.
- Business errors on the part of the franchisor that can affect you and your profits.
- The sometimes difficult task of assessing a potential franchisor, especially a new one.
- Dependency on the franchisor, which may be total.

What can happen when franchisor and franchisee don't see eye to eye? One story we've heard concerns a large restaurant franchise which advertises heavily on national TV. We've all heard the phrase, "At *participating* _____ restaurants." While it's quite true that participation is voluntary for whatever's being touted (free french fries with every double cheeseburger, for example) some franchisees who didn't "volunteer," found the truck delivering supplies from the franchisor suddenly breaking down and arriving later and later.

The second tale of woe comes from the owner of a franchised eye-care business—one offering examinations, glasses, and accessories. One day, without warning, a team of people from "the home office" descended on this business demanding to see the books. After hanging around for two days, the team presented the franchisee with a bill for $11,000 representing unpaid royalties and a fee for their audit. The franchisee was furious because he believed he was paying the proper amounts and also because he had been intimidated in his own establishment.

SUMMARY

Now we know what a franchise is and what it isn't. In its simplest form, it's a legal agreement between two parties wherein each party gives up some legal rights to gain some others. In the best arrangements, everyone wins. The franchisor expands its number of outlets and gains additional income; the franchisee has a business of his or her own which is as close to a guaranteed success as we can get in an uncertain world.

We've looked at franchising and know what makes it tick. Now let's take a look at you. In the next chapter we'll see if you have the right stuff to be a successful franchisee.

CHAPTER 3

Are You Franchise Material?

INITIAL CONSIDERATIONS

There are many ways to make a living in this country. Being an independent business owner is one of those ways and it's certainly not for everyone. Although there are always exceptions to every rule, being in business for yourself successfully requires certain personal characteristics and skills. There are also certain needs each of us may seek to fulfill via our work as we can see from the following diagram.

The spectrum demonstrates the balance between two variables—the need for security and the need for independence. It doesn't show that entrepreneurs, categories 8, 9, and 10, are "better" than their government counterparts in categories 1, 2, and 3; it simply indicates that their needs are different. Look at the diagram carefully and put yourself in category 8, the person who buys a franchise. Does this seem about right for

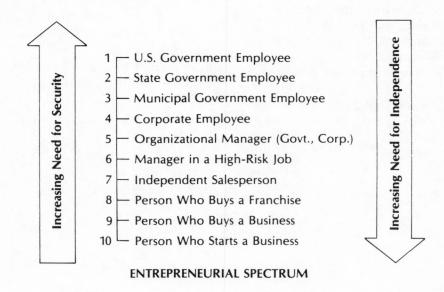

1	—	U.S. Government Employee
2	—	State Government Employee
3	—	Municipal Government Employee
4	—	Corporate Employee
5	—	Organizational Manager (Govt., Corp.)
6	—	Manager in a High-Risk Job
7	—	Independent Salesperson
8	—	Person Who Buys a Franchise
9	—	Person Who Buys a Business
10	—	Person Who Starts a Business

ENTREPRENEURIAL SPECTRUM

you? If you feel you need more independence and can tolerate higher risk, then perhaps you should instead think about buying an existing business or starting one of your own.

Maury O'Connell, vice president of franchise development for On Line Computer Centers, Inc., gives us more insight into the personality of the successful franchisee. (The following is from a copyrighted issue of *Marketing News;* the article is entitled "Like love, franchising can bloom or turn sour," by Mike Major.) Mr. O'Connell assesses prospective franchisees using a 1-to-10 rating scale.

"If a person scores a one, I know he's so security conscious that even though he fantasizes about going into business for himself, he'll never really be able to cut himself loose from the umbilical cord of his job," O'Connell says. "We need risk takers."

"But if he's at the other end of the scale, I know he's so independent an entrepreneur that he won't take directions well and will argue with every aspect of our system. About six or seven is what I'm looking for, a person willing to take a risk but also willing to work in harmony with a supporting system."

In other words, you may get into the safest franchise in the world, but if you have the wrong attitude you may fail in that business.

What's a "wrong" attitude or reason for going into a particular business? Here are a few to consider:

1. Ego trips. Using a business to give some kind of status or false prestige.
2. Revenge. There are cases of men and women getting into their own businesses just to get back at someone, usually a former employer. We've even seen a case or two where an ex-spouse was the target.

3. Last-ditch stand. Once in a while we find folks getting into business because they can't find a job. They're really people who should be employed, rather than self-employed.
4. Fantasy. One of us lives in northern New England and sees this regularly. A person or couple from Boston or New York decides how lovely it would be to have a franchise in the country. However, what's popular with the yuppies may not make it with the rural folk.
5. Greed. Combine this one with the first item, ego trips, and you have an absolutely unbeatable formula for failure. No doubt about it. Successful business owners get their kicks from their independence, not their bank balances.

Let's comment just a bit more on the issue of money. Don't get us wrong: you can make lots of money in many franchised businesses, especially if you own more than one. Those who see only profit as their goal miss much of the fun and excitement running your own business has to offer. After a while just making money becomes pretty boring.

Now get yourself a pencil because it's time for a quiz.

PERSONAL ASSESSMENT

In the pages ahead, we're going to give you an opportunity to assess your personality and business skills. The purpose of this evaluation isn't to point out "right" versus "wrong" characteristics, but rather to make you aware of your starting point—what you are or have right now. Needless to say, the results will be meaningless unless you are totally honest with yourself. Check the block that most aptly applies to you.

1. Are your willing to take moderate risks in life to achieve the goals you want? (Please notice the word "moderate". Business owners aren't crap shooters.)
   - □ Yes
   - □ No
   - □ Uncertain

2. Can you operate within an environment that is somewhat ill-defined and may even, from time to time, be chaotic?
   - □ Yes
   - □ No
   - □ Uncertain

3. Do you possess the drive and energy to work long hours to achieve what you want?
   - □ Yes
   - □ No
   - □ Uncertain

4. Are you prepared to place the needs of your business above those of your friends, your family, your community?
☐ Yes
☐ No
☐ Uncertain

5. Are you the kind of person who can take full responsibility for both your successes and your failures?
☐ Yes
☐ No
☐ Uncertain

6. Are your failures merely learning experiences for you?
☐ Yes
☐ No
☐ Uncertain

7. Are you comfortable having someone else in control of your working environment?
☐ Yes
☐ No
☐ Uncertain

8. Are you comfortable around strangers?
☐ Yes
☐ No
☐ Uncertain

9. Can you say "no" to someone you believe is trying to get you to do something that you don't want to do?
☐ Yes
☐ No
☐ Uncertain

10. When the need arises, can you tackle and complete a job that may not interest you?
☐ Yes
☐ No
☐ Uncertain

11. Are you willing to work hard to acquire new skills?
☐ Yes
☐ No
☐ Uncertain

12. Can you lead and inspire others?
☐ Yes
☐ No
☐ Uncertain

13. Can you take harsh criticism, even on a personal level?
☐ Yes
☐ No
☐ Uncertain

14. Are you able to take orders gracefully?
☐ Yes
☐ No
☐ Uncertain

For the next six statements, check the box that reflects your feelings.

15. It's more important to accomplish what I want than to earn a great deal of money.
☐ Agree
☐ Disagree
☐ Uncertain

16. People learn more from their mistakes than they do from their successes.
☐ Agree
☐ Disagree
☐ Uncertain

17. "Slow and steady wins the race."

☐ Agree
☐ Disagree
☐ Uncertain

18. It isn't necessary to cut corners or compromise in order to succeed.

☐ Agree
☐ Disagree
☐ Uncertain

19. I value intangible qualities like love and wisdom over money and possessions.

☐ Agree
☐ Disagree
☐ Uncertain

20. There is no other person I would rather be than me at this moment.

☐ Agree
☐ Disagree
☐ Uncertain

To score this self-assessment, give five points for every "Yes" or "Agree," three points for every "Uncertain," and zero for "No" or "Disagree." Your total score will be between 0 and 100; you can give yourself a letter grade:

90–100: A
80–89: B
70–79: C
60–69: D
below 60: F

Let's now move into some areas that will enable you to think about your desires and skills in the business area. The first of these checklists gives you an opportunity to set down some of the beginning criteria for your new franchise. If you're unclear about some of these items, leave them blank for now, but keep in mind that they should be settled in the future. The second list will enable you to assess the skills that are important in running any kind of business. If you find there are large gaps in your business skills, you may need to acquire more knowledge and experience. Be sure to find out how much *business* training is offered by the franchisor, especially if you're weak in certain areas.

Business Criteria

1. Where will this business be located (town, state)?

2. When will I begin the business (month, year)? (*Note:* Even if you are highly uncertain of your timing, estimate as closely as possible.)

3. My business must eventually have the following characteristics: (*Note:* These could be measurable quantities like sales of $500,000 or intangible items such as quality.)
   a.
   b.
   c.
   d.
   e.

4. My business must *not* have the following characteristics:
   a.
   b.
   c.
   d.
   e.

5. Here is a list of franchises (restaurant, office service firm, equipment rental) that are appealing to me:
   a.
   b.
   c.
   d.
   e.

6. Here is a list of franchises that don't appeal to me:
   a.
   b.
   c.
   d.
   e.

7. My lifestyle demands I earn the following annual salary: $_____

8. I eventually want to work _____ hours per week:
   ☐ less than 20
   ☐ 20 to 40
   ☐ 40 to 60
   ☐ 60 to 80
   ☐ more than 80

9. Which of the following best applies to me? (More than one could apply):
   ☐ I want a small franchise and want to keep it small.
   ☐ I want a franchise that is initially large or one that will grow.
   ☐ I want to own several franchises.
   ☐ I want to run the business for the rest of my life if possible.
   ☐ I want to develop the business, then sell it.
   ☐ Other. Specify:

10. Who do I want as my primary customer(s)?
    ☐ The consumer (the general public)
    ☐ Other businesses or industry
    ☐ Professional organizations (accountants, lawyers)
    ☐ Non-profit organizations (YMCAs, churches)
    ☐ Special groups (farmers, pilots)
       ☐ Specify:

    ☐ State or local government
    ☐ Federal government
    ☐ Foreign (export)
    ☐ Other. Specify:

11. What kind of a franchise business meets my general needs and requirements
   □ Retail
   □ Wholesale
   □ Service
   □ Transportation
   □ Construction
   □ Manufacturing
   □ Other. Specify:

12. Will there be others starting this business with you?
   □ No
   □ Yes
   If yes, list person(s) and relationship (friend, spouse) if any:

   Name   Relationship
   a.
   b.
   c.

13. Who will be my advisors?

   Name   Address
   a. Attorney
   b. Accountant
   c. Insurance Agent
   d. Consultant
   e. Other

14. How do I want to sell my products or services?
   □ Me
   □ Employed salespeople
   □ Sales representatives (non-employees)
   □ Distributors/dealers
   □ Mail
   □ Other. Specify:

15. List below any assured income from trust, real estate investments, and the like:

   Source   Estimated Annual Income
   a.
   b.
   c.

16. Make a list below of any relatives or friends who might be approached for money later on:

   Name   Relationship
   a.
   b.
   c.
   d.
   e.

17. What are my important reasons for wanting to own my own business? (Note: More than one may apply.)
- ☐ Believe I can "do it better" than existing competition.
- ☐ It's a dream. (No negative intent.)
- ☐ Don't like where I live now.
- ☐ Want to make a lot of money.
- ☐ Want independence.
- ☐ Quit my job.
- ☐ Was fired.
- ☐ Fed up with corporate life.
- ☐ Want legacy for my children.
- ☐ Need tax shelter.
- ☐ Want to prove myself.
- ☐ Can't get along with bosses.
- ☐ Have unused talent.
- ☐ Want to do it my way without compromise.
- ☐ Want to be of real service to others.
- ☐ Family can work together.
- ☐ Other. Specify:

18. What are my major reservations about being in business?
- ☐ Fear of failure.
- ☐ Lack of business knowledge.
- ☐ Too much work.
- ☐ Giving up present pay and benefits.
- ☐ Leaving/losing present friends.
- ☐ No time for family.
- ☐ Giving up present outside activities.
- ☐ Might get locked in.
- ☐ Lack of confidence.
- ☐ Not enough money of my own.
- ☐ Not knowing where to turn for help.
- ☐ Acting impulsively.
- ☐ Acting too slowly.
- ☐ Fear of success.
- ☐ The entire question of risk.
- ☐ Fear of change.
- ☐ Discomfort with ill-defined situation—the unknown.
- ☐ Other. Specify:

19. What makes me think this franchise will succeed as a *business?* (*Note:* Only answer this and the next question if you've already looked at a particular franchise.)
- ☐ Location.
- ☐ Product or service.
- ☐ People on my team.
- ☐ Fills special market need.
- ☐ Others have done it.
- ☐ Have time to do it right.
- ☐ Low capital requirements.
- ☐ Other. Specify:

20. What are the weaknesses of this business as I see it now?

□ Location.
□ Product or service.
□ People on my team.
□ Limited market.
□ Heavy capital requirements.

□ Stiff competition.
□ Idea too new or untried.
□ Legal requirements.
□ Other. Specify:

SKILLS CHECKLIST
I believe I have sufficient knowledge and background to run my own business.

Business Skill	*Yes*	*No*	*Uncertain*

I. SALES AND MARKETING
  A. Marketing Research—Discovering market conditions and analyzing customer demand.
  B. Marketing Planning—Using marketing research to construct strategy necessary to reach the market.
  C. Pricing—Setting final prices that will be profitable but not out of reach of the customer.
  D. Advertising/Public Relations—Using both message and media in a proper balance to increase customer demand and awareness.
  E. Sales Management—Supervising others in the selling process.
  F. Personal Selling—Am I or can I be an effective salesperson?
  G. Sales Administration—Knowledge of marketing law.
  H. Competitive Analysis—Keeping abreast of what my competition is doing.

II. BUSINESS OPERATION
  A. Purchasing—Knowing how to buy goods and service at minimum prices and best terms.
  B. Inventory Control—Keeping supplies and raw materials at levels that are neither too high nor too low.
  C. Scheduling—When to schedule certain events in a business for maximum effectiveness: a sense of timing.

SKILLS CHECKLIST

I believe I have sufficient knowledge and
background to run my own business.

Business Skill	*Yes*	*No*	*Uncertain*

      D. Quality Control—How much effort to expend toward assuring proper quality consistent with price and customer expectation.

      E. Business Planning—How to prepare and follow a business plan.

      F. Expansion—Knowing how to plan for and use growth without running out of control.

III. FINANCE

      A. Bookkeeping—The recording of accounting information in journals and ledgers.

      B. Accounting—Understanding the key financial statements of a business, the income statement, and the balance sheet.

      C. Budgeting—Doing a cash flow projection and using deviations to analyze estimated vs. actual performance.

      D. Cost Control—Not only being able to detect excess expenses but doing something about it.

      E. Credit & Collection—Knowing the proper circumstances in which to extend or deny credit and being able to collect overdue accounts.

      F. Raising Money—Ability to deal with banks and other financial sources to secure capital.

      G. Banking Relations—Knowing what banks expect from a small business.

      H. Breakeven Analysis—How to do it; what it means.

      I. Ratio Analysis—Using financial ratios to further assess information on the income statement and balance sheet.

      J. Taxes—A basic understanding of the difference between personal and business taxes.

SKILLS CHECKLIST
I believe I have sufficient knowledge and
background to run my own business.

Business Skill	Yes	No	Uncertain

IV. ADMINISTRATION
    A. Team Building—Selecting team members, hiring, firing, training, motivating, and leading.
    B. Personnel Policies—Pay and benefits, labor guidelines, tax withholding, payroll reports (federal and state).
    C. Dealing with Professionals—Accountants, attorneys, consultants, the SBA.
    D. Using Information—Where to get information and how to put it to proper use.
    E. Technology—The use of devices such as small business computers and word processors.
    F. Business Law—A basic understanding of what is legal and illegal.

TOTALS   _____   _____   _____

Note: There are 30 items in the skills checklist. You should have a *minimum* of 15 in the "YES" column.

Congratulations! You've just completed three crucial exercises about yourself and your potential franchise. If you've been honest, you now have a fair idea where you're headed, what you've got to help get you there, and what additional knowledge skills, and information you need. Again, no one ever has everything they need in any small business and in a way that's part of the fun.

Go back now and review what you've learned from the three exercises. In the first one, the Personal Assessment, you gave yourself a letter grade. If that grade was a "D" or an "F," examine the categories in which you didn't answer "yes" or "agree." Make a list of those personal items where you fall short and then ask yourself what barriers and beliefs stand in your way for making changes. The second exercise dealt with business criteria: if a large number of the questions were left blank, then you are probably some time away from having a franchised business of your own. Look carefully at the items you need to resolve, and work on resolving them. Finally, you completed a skills checklist with four categories—sales and marketing, business operation, finance, and administration. See if any of those categories have a majority of "no" and "uncertain" checks. If so, this should lead you to consider additional study in those areas. For example, if your knowledge of finance is weak, you may want to take a standard two-semester college course in accounting. Don't start your own business until you've satisfied *yourself* that you're ready, both personally and professionally. And don't forget to check the level and type of training provided by the franchisor. You might discover, for instance, that although you have little or no knowledge of business operation (purchasing, inventory control) the franchisor will train you in those areas.

YOUR FINANCES

You need money to get into a franchise. How much money? And for what? Let's look at the second question first. Generally you need money for three things:

1. The franchise fee. Although we'll go into fees in more detail later, the franchise fee is essentially a one-time payment to acquire the franchise name and a license to use the franchisor's process. Franchise fees can vary from a few hundred dollars to over $100,000.
2. Supplies, equipment, inventory which you may be required to buy from the franchisor or an approved source.
3. Enough operating capital to sustain the business during its early months of establishment. The franchisor should estimate this for you; be wary if he or she won't.

Most franchisees don't purchase any real estate for their business. Normally they lease their own space or, in a few cases, lease the location from the franchisor.

Before you approach a franchisor regarding the purchase of a franchise, you need to know two things: your net worth and what you need to live on. Both values are vitally important so we're going to help you calculate them step by step. Let's begin with your net worth, what you're worth in dollars and cents.

In a net worth statement you assign a monetary value to the things you own (assets), the things you owe (liabilities), and subtract the liabilities from the assets; the result is your net worth. If your liabilities are greater than your assets, your net worth will be negative and you will be in a *technical* state known as insolvency. You're not bankrupt—that's a *legal* state resulting from a ruling of a federal bankruptcy court.

A net worth statement, like the balance sheet of a business, shows what happens if you convert all your assets to cash and pay off all your liabilities. Ideally, you're left with a bunch of money. It's important to analyze this because if you're like most people who get into a franchise, you're going to use some or most of your assets (cash in life insurance policies, a mutual fund, part of your pension) to get into business. You still may not have all the funds you need and therefore may need to turn to the franchisor, a commercial bank, or both for additional funding. Therefore, whether or not it turns out you have all the cash you need, your net worth analysis is critical. You need it to show you where you are financially, and potential funding sources need it to evaluate your needs.

You can use the form on the next page to determine your net worth. First, notice a net worth statement has a date on it; this is because it represents a snapshot of your financial condition at a specific moment in time, a frozen frame, if you will. If today is Tuesday, June 9, 1987, your finances will be different from next Tuesday, June 16th. In the intervening week you may deposit a paycheck in your checking account, increase your net worth; or, maybe the 100 shares of Engulf and Devour that you own drop five points, decreasing your net worth by $500. Note that assets are on the left and liabilities on the right. This is merely convention—there's no magic to this alignment.

Let's start with the asset (left) side. When recording amounts, don't worry about getting figures to the nearest penny. If you're within $50 of the exact figure, that's good enough.

Cash on Hand: This means greens in your jeans, or, as grandfather used to say, cash money. Although most people don't carry a lot of money around with them, some folks keep cash hidden in piggy banks and the like. So, if you have some mad money stashed away in a coffee can or a mattress, include it.

Cash in Banks: Next to real cash money, funds in banks are the next best thing. Figure your actual checking account(s) balance for the day you choose to do your net worth statement. If you haven't balanced your checking account, do it now. If you have a savings account, or several, call the bank and ask them to calculate any interest due. (In the category called "Other" you may have certificates of deposit, CDs. Again, it's important to include any accrued interest on CDs; your local banking officer or head teller can give you this information.)

Money Market: In the late 1970s when interest rates reached 20 percent, many people performed disintermediation, that is, switching funds from one source

Net Worth Statement of _____

as of _____ 19____

Assets		Liabilities	
Cash on hand	$_____	Notes payable to banks	
Cash in banks		Secured	$_____
Checking	_____	Unsecured	_____
Savings	_____	Amounts payable to others	
Other	_____	Secured	_____
Money Market	_____	Unsecured	_____
U.S. Government securities	_____	Accounts due	
Marketable securities		Credit cards	_____
Stocks	_____	Installment loans	_____
Bonds	_____	Other	_____
Mutual Funds	_____		
Other	_____		
Receivables	_____		
Life Insurance (CSV)	_____	Unpaid taxes	_____
Real Estate	_____	Insurance loans	_____
Vehicles	_____	Mortgages	_____
Personal property	_____	Other debts	_____
Pension benefits			
	_____	TOTAL LIABILITIES	$_____
Business Interests	_____	NET WORTH	$_____
Other Assets	_____		
		LIABILITIES AND	
TOTAL ASSETS	$_____	NET WORTH	$_____

(bank savings accounts) to another, the new money market funds. If you still have one of these, write in the balance as well as any accrued interest.

U.S. Government Securities: There seems to be hundreds of kinds of government securities—treasury notes, treasury bonds, Series E bonds, Series H bonds, Fannie Maes, Ginnie Maes, repos, treasury bills, and on and on. If you have any of these, put down their present values.

Marketable Securities: For stocks—both common and preferred—give their market value on the date of the net worth statement. If you own stock in a company that's not publicly traded, you'll need to determine its value. If you own restricted stock, it's better not to assign any value to it at all because it's not "marketable." Bonds include such items as convertible debentures, corporate bonds, municipal bonds, and the like. For mutual funds, you need what's called the net asset value (NAV) which you can determine by checking the Wall Street Journal. (For the category called "Other" you should include

any items such as options [puts and calls], commodity contracts, foreign bonds, margin accounts; remember, though, they must be *marketable*.)

Receivables: If any person or business owes you money, it's a receivable and usually consists of loans receivable and notes receivable, the latter being represented in writing.

Life Insurance (CSV): CSV stands for cash surrender value. You may need to call your insurance agent to obtain the correct figure.

Real Estate: If you own a house, some land, or have an interest in something like a real estate investment trust, you need to determine the fair market value; that may require appraisal by a professional.

Vehicles: For any automobiles, motorcycles, trucks, snowmobiles, motor homes, boats, airplanes, you need to determine the current fair market value. You can probably get these figures from an installment loan officer at your local bank.

Personal Property: Be careful with items in this category. There's a tendency to throw furniture and appliances in at either their cost when you bought them or their replacement cost. Unless you have a precious oriental rug or a valuable silver collection, value your belongings at what they'd bring at a yard sale. Be certain, though, to include things like coin or stamp collections.

Pension Benefits: If you work for an employer, you may have vested rights in a pension plan. Check with your personnel director. Also include any value of IRAs or Keoughs you have.

Business Interests: If you have a small business of your own, there may be value in the venture. Check with your accountant. If you value it yourself, be very, *very* conservative.

Other Assets: Usually people will list the value of trusts under other assets. Don't list contingent assets; if you're named in rich Aunt Sadie's will that has no value until her demise. Other categories might include such items as tax rebates due, insurance dividends, profit-sharing.

Add up the assets and put the result under Total Assets. Surprised? Many people are, but before you go off on some spree, remember, we're going to start listing liabilities, which accountants call claims against assets. Let's start with the right hand column. As with assets, we aren't going to deal with *contingent* liabilities. For example, you might be a co-maker or co-guarantor on a car loan for your sister, and if she defaults and can't pay, you'll have to. Liability only occurs if she fails to make the payments, and therefore it doesn't belong on a net worth statement. Make, however, a separate list of any contingent liabilities (co-endorser of a note, a lien against some asset such as real estate) because a bank will ask for that information if you apply for a loan.

Notes Payable to Banks: This category doesn't include either mortgages or car loans but represents a note in writing which is either secured (i.e., backed by an asset of some kind) or unsecured.

Amounts Payable to Others: This might be a loan by your brother-in-law, a credit union loan, or other personal debts.

Accounts Due: Under the first category, *credit cards,* list all open balances on VISA, MasterCard, gasoline credit cards, Sears, Wards, and the like. In the *installment loan* category, total up things like car loans, loans on pleasure vehicles. Do not show items that you pay for as a service, like telephone or cable TV.

Unpaid Taxes: List any taxes due on both income and property. Pro-rate any property taxes. For instance, if you actually pay real estate taxes on your home at the end of every year, meaning you don't have a tax escrow account, and this is June, put down one-half of the established annual tax.

Insurance Loans: If you have borrowed against your life insurance, figure in the total amount you've borrowed. Note that if on the asset side you put down *net* CSV (total CSV less outstanding loans), leave this item blank.

Mortgages: Show the *principal* balance (not any interest) of all mortgages.

Other Debts: This category is a catch-all and includes medical bills, a pledge you have made to a charitable organization, a legal judgment. Again, don't show normal operating expenses here.

Add up all your debts and obligations and put the sum under total liabilities. Next, subtract total liabilities from total assets; the result is your net worth. Then add total liabilities to net worth to give liabilities and net worth which should equal total assets. Now you can celebrate (we hope).

What you just did in arriving at your net worth is to figure out the absolute maximum amount of cash you can lay your hands on if you get rid of everything that you own and owe. The chances of your doing that are next to zero, but you now have an idea of sources you can tap for your business. If you're a year or even two away, you'll have to update your net worth statement; but once you've done it the first time, subsequent calculations are a piece of cake.

Now that you know something about your net worth, you must estimate monthly living expenses. Determining how much money you need to live on is a vital step, not just an academic exercise. Too many people say that to be self-employed, they're willing to live in a hovel, eat curds and whey, and drive a 10-year-old car. Although some may make adjustments here and there, most people who adopt a certain lifestyle maintain that lifesyle. You should not put yourself in a position of extreme personal sacrifice. A business should provide a certain standard of living, and if it doesn't, you may feel that the whole escapade isn't worth the time and effort. We did say earlier that *good* entrepreneurs don't pursue personal wealth as an end product, but they do understand economic values. If a business can't pay you a fair salary, then it's not a business, it's a hobby.

On the next page is a form to estimate your current monthly expenses. As you begin working closely with a franchisor, he or she should be able to estimate how much money you can make from your business. It's certainly important to know if that amount is enough to meet your needs. Any business should provide three types of financial "return" to the business owner:

1. A fair salary comparable to that of a manager of that kind of business.
2. A return for the risk of enterprise.
3. Sufficient cash flow to fund the business's assets.

The monthly expenses statement is self-explanatory; remember, however, you'll have to adjust some expenses to get them on a monthly rather than a weekly basis. For instance, if your average food bill is $60 per week, then you need to multiply by 4⅓ or 4.33 to reflect a monthly level:

$$\$60 \times 4.33 = \$260/month$$

Similarly, if your real estate taxes are $1200 annually, you will need to divide by 12:

$$\frac{\$1,200}{12} = \$100/month$$

Now let's summarize what you've discovered and what it means to your business. Your net worth statement tells you the maximum amount of money you could raise from your personal assets, but you'll certainly not want to use all of it. It's a good idea to earmark which assets will be converted to cash. Once you do this, you will have an amount of money that represents your personal investment in the business.

We hope this assessment of your personal abilities and financial status was both interesting and informative. By taking the time and making the effort necessary to complete each section as thoroughly and honestly as possible, you'll be better prepared than 90 percent of those who choose to follow the franchised route. By being better prepared, you increase your chances of success and decrease the chance of any surprises that might negatively affect you or your new business. Carefully compiling the information suggested may very well be *the* ounce of prevention that saves you a lot of headaches in the future.

Now that you know what you want, where your strengths and weaknesses lie, how much you can afford to spend, and how much you need to earn, let's see what franchisors offer and how this may or may not be compatible with what you want and need.

ESTIMATED MONTHLY EXPENSES

Item	Amount
Food	$ _____
Housing	
a. Monthly payment or rent	_____
b. Taxes	_____
c. Insurance	_____
d. Repairs and maintenance	_____
Clothing	_____
Auto	
a. Payment	_____
b. Gasoline	_____
c. Repairs	_____
d. Insurance, fees, taxes	_____
Utilities	
a. Electricity	_____
b. Heat, hot water (if not electric)	_____
c. Telephone	_____
d. Other (water, gas)	_____
Credit cards (not covered elsewhere)	_____
Installment and other loans	_____
Life Insurance	_____
Travel and entertainment	_____
Donations	_____
Medical and dental	_____
Investment and savings	_____
Miscellaneous	_____
TOTAL	$

CHAPTER 4

Which Franchise Is for You?

In this chapter we'll be discussing some of the different kinds of franchising available and how to find out about them. In order to make the most of this material, you may want to consider arming yourself with two additional references, each costing less than $10.00. The first is the U.S. Department of Commerce (USDC) "Franchise Opportunities Handbook." It's published annually and is available from the Superintendent of Documents, U.S. Government Printing Office, Washington, DC 20402.

The second reference, complimentary to the first, is the "Directory of Membership" available from the International Franchise Association (IFA), 1025 Connecticut Avenue, N.W., Suite 707, Washington, DC 20036. This is also an annual publication and costs about $7.00.

The *Franchise Opportunities Handbook* lists the names of over 1,000 franchisors and gives:

1. The name and address of the company.
2. A brief description of the operation.
3. The number of operating franchises.
4. Year of inception.
5. Equity capital needed.
6. Any financial assistance available.
7. Whether training is provided.
8. Whether managerial assistance is available.
9. Date the information was submitted.

It also provides other sources of government assistance (Department of Commerce and Small Business Administration offices, books, pamphlets) for potential franchisors. The International Franchise Association publication includes valuable hints for would-be franchisees and lists the 300 or so members of the IFA. Neither publication can assure you success as a franchisee of one of the listed firms, but at least you know these companies have some kind of track record. We strongly recommend the addition of both references to your basic business library.

TYPES OF BUSINESSES

With the exception of businesses such as farming, fishing or forestry, most businesses fall into one of six general categories:

1. *Retail.* A retail business sells things to the consumer. This category includes fast-food restaurants but also stores of all kinds—hardware, hot tubs, appliances, electronics, auto parts, pets, paint, drugs, clothing—nearly any kind you can imagine. In a franchised retail business the franchise buys goods (often directly from the franchisor) and resells them. To succeed in retail you should enjoy working with the general public.

2. *Service.* Although retailing dominates franchising, the service category is growing more rapidly. A service franchise doesn't require the large investment in inventory that's necessary in retail. However, you may have to consider obtaining a license because businesses such as employment agencies, real estate firms, and beauty parlors are regulated in many states. Many potential franchisees convert a skill they acquired working for someone else into their own service business. For example, suppose you spent six years with the local landscape company and enjoy lawn work, but want your own business. There are about 10 national franchisors in the lawn and garden business you might consider.

There's a wide range of service franchises available from campgrounds to furniture refinishing, dental practices to tax services, computer dating to miniature golf.

3. *Construction.* There seem to be three general subclasses within this rather small category of franchises. The first includes those franchises engaged in the total construction of homes and buildings. Franchisees of New England Log Homes of Hamden, Connecticut, erect model log homes which then serve as the office from which they sell their product to prospective buyers. The second franchised construction group sells products for already existing houses and buildings. Perma-Jack Company franchisees sell building foundation stabilizing systems whereas Poraflor franchisees, as the name implies, offer "seamless" flooring. The third group of construction franchisors includes renovators and remodelers, such as GNU Services Corp. which specializes in porcelain and fiberglass repair and refinishing.

4. *Manufacturing.* With the exception of soft-drink bottlers, there are practically no manufacturing franchises. What usually occurs in this industry group is licensing rather than franchising. You perfect a machine or process to make something and let me use it if I pay you a royalty. You don't control my business and our relationship isn't as close as that between franchisor and franchisee.

5. *Wholesale.* At last check there were less than five wholesaling franchises, and they required very specialized knowledge, such as how to sell used machine tools.

6. *Transportation.* This general business category doesn't exist in franchising because vehicle rental franchises (Hertz, Avis) are classified as service businesses, not transportation.

So it's most likely you'll be heading for either a retail or service franchise. Although we presented a list of franchises in Chapter 2, let's specifically examine the retail and service categories. Studying these lists is very important, especially if you haven't chosen the kind of franchise you want. We've left a space next to each business category for you to check those which appeal to you. You may also find it helpful to rank-order the businesses, designating the most appealing business as "1," your second choice as "2," and so on.

Retail Franchises
Food
    Donuts
    Grocery and Specialty Stores   ____
    Ice Cream, Yogurt, Candy, Popcorn   ____
    Pancakes, Waffles, and Pretzels   ____
    Restaurants—Drive-In & Carry-Out
      (fast-food, mostly)   ____
Automotive
    Shocks, Mufflers, and Brakes   ____
    Transmissions   ____
    General Service and Tune-Up   ____
    Rustproofing   ____
    Auto Parts   ____
    Auto Cleaning and Polishing   ____
    Lubrication   ____
    Body Work   ____
Stores
    Children's   ____
    Clothing and Shoes   ____
    Drug and Health Goods   ____
    Cosmetics and Toiletries   ____
    General Merchandise   ____
    Optical Products   ____
    Paint and Decorating   ____
    Hardware   ____
    Video/Audio   ____
    Computer   ____
    Electronics   ____
    Art   ____
    Sporting Goods   ____
    Tapes and Records   ____
    Appliances   ____
    Camera   ____
    Frames and Pictures   ____
    Clocks   ____
    Building Supplies   ____
    Books   ____
    Flowers   ____
    Pets and Animals   ____
    Gift   ____

Service Franchises
  Professional*
    Legal   ——
    Dental   ——
    Medical   ——
  Personal Services
    Taxes   ——
    Beauty and Hair   ——
    Health (non-medical, such as exercise)   ——
    Education   ——
    Cleaning (home)   ——
    Real Estate   ——
    Travel   ——
    Lawn and Garden   ——
    Insurance   ——
    Water Conditioning   ——
    Recreation   ——
    Campgrounds   ——
    Pest Control   ——
    Hotels and Motels   ——
    Laundry and Drycleaning   ——
  Rental
    Auto and Truck   ——
    Equipment   ——
  Business Services
    Printing and Copying   ——
    Computer Services   ——
    Taxes and Accounting   ——
    Business Consulting   ——
    Maintenance and Cleaning   ——
    Mail Services and Freight   ——
    Business Brokerage   ——
    Insurance and Appraisal   ——
    Employment   ——
    Telephone   ——
    Investigations and Security   ——
    First Aid and Safety   ——
  Education

Our list is not exhaustive but it will give you some idea of what's available versus your personal interests. Now let's look at the best way to find a franchisor.

FINDING FRANCHISORS

There are many ways to find out about franchisors. Do you remember what happened to Mary

*NOTE: You usually need to be a practitioner in these fields to qualify.

Knolls, who responded to a one-time ad in her local paper? What happened to Mary is sufficiently common that we're going to tell you to be extremely suspicious of any franchisor's ad in a local paper and all those with phrases like

"Investment opportunity of a lifetime."
"Instant profit."
"Earn a million in your first three years."

or those with the kiss of death ending:

"Mr. Schwartz will be at your local Holiday Inn on Tuesday from 9 to 5."

Stay totally away from that one!

Where can you find out about legitimate franchisors? Every Thursday the *Wall Street Journal* focuses on franchise opportunities, doing the best job it can to screen possible fly-by-nights. But even the *Journal* can't be perfect. The trick is to follow the ads for several weeks; the hit-and-run artists usually can't afford to run an ad in a major paper for a long time.

In a recent Thursday *Journal* we saw the following display ads; most of the names are indicative of the kind of business being franchised:

International House of Pancakes
Sylvan Learning Corporation
Accountants Microsystems Inc.
Entré Computer Centers
General Business Services
AAMCO Transmissions, Inc.
Cucos Mexican Restaurante
ValCom Computer Centers
Taco Bell Corp.
Health Force (We couldn't figure out what they did from the ad.)
Tidy Car Inc.
Kwik-Kopy Corp.
Maytag HOME STYLE Laundry
Print Shack
Mailhouse, Inc, (direct mail)
Cottman Transmission Systems, Inc.
Snelling & Snelling (employment agency)
Alpha Graphics Printshops
Fantastic Sam's (hair care)
Budget Instant Printing Centers
Ponderosa Steakhouse
National Video Inc.

VR Business Brokers
Meineke Discount Muffler Shops
Management Recruiters International
International Tours Inc.
MicroAge Computer Stores
PIP Instant Printing
Sir Speedy Printing Centers

The list is laden with restaurants, computer stores, automotive services, and copy centers; and the mix changes each week.

Should you only depend on Thursday's *Journal?* Not necessarily. The Sunday *New York Times'* business section is also a good source of information, as are the newspapers of other *large* cities. As we said before, stay away from small-town papers in general; reputable, established franchisors rarely use them.

Magazines can also be a source of information about possible franchise opportunities. Three magazines for small business owners—*Inc., In Business,* and *Venture*—offer such information. These are available at most large newsstands or you might consider subscribing to one or all three. It is also worthwhile to visit a library and check other magazines such as *Popular Science, Popular Mechanics,* and some of the publications for retired people.

There are also franchising periodicals. You may be able to get a sample back issue from the publisher, if these aren't available in your local library.

The American Franchise   (Quarterly)
530 Valley Forge Plaza
King of Prussia, PA 19406

Franchising Today   (Bimonthly)
Franchise Technologies, Inc.
1201 San Luis Obispo Road
Hayward, CA 94544

Franchising/Investments Around the World   (Monthly)
National Association of Franchise Companies
Box 610097
North Miami, FL 33161

Franchising World   (Monthly)
International Franchise Association
1025 Connecticut Avenue, N.W.
Washington, DC 20036

You may also want to subscribe to the newsletter:

The Info Franchise Newsletter
Info Press
736 Center Street
Lewiston, NY 14092

There are also franchise trade shows held every year in the larger cities of the United States and some of the periodicals on franchising list their locations. Be a tad careful of the shows, however, because a great deal of "hustling" can go on.

WHERE YOU ARE NOW

What we've done so far is paint some of the plusses and minuses of franchising, let you assess yourself as a potential franchisee, describe the basic business categories, and give you some sources of additional information. However, before you're ready to contact a franchisor in person, by mail, or by phone you need more background. We aren't suggesting that the more than 2,000 franchisors in this country are sleazy or unethical—most aren't; however, many new franchises often get going without the appropriate marketing research. For example, some franchised tanning salons and hot tub spas turned out to be short-term fads rather than sound, long-term business endeavors. One question to ask yourself: "Will this business satisfy a *continuing* need?" Certainly people need to eat, have their cars fixed, and their taxes figured. (Assuming, of course, that the government won't simplify the tax laws—which seems most unlikely.) And certainly many Americans are concerned about their looks, health, and productive use of their time. Although regularly lying under ultra-violet lights gave them the tanned look of health, the tan fad faded quickly when scientists linked skin cancer to excessive exposure, and rigorous exercising replaced lounging about as the acceptable form of leisure time activity. For those owning franchised tanning businesses, the financial outlook went from sunny to bleak very quickly. Therefore, consider the longevity of the business you're thinking about, not just its appeal to a lot of people right now.

Now you're ready to make that initial contact with the franchisor, and next we'll discuss what you can expect.

CHAPTER 5

Initial Contacts:
What To Expect

INITIAL CONTACTS

Right now you probably have either a general franchise category (retail, service) in mind or have focused on more specific franchised areas (computer store, accounting practice). And chances are you discovered potential franchises from:

- An article or ad in the popular press or a national magazine.
- An existing franchisee.
- Source material (IFA's membership list for example).
- Specialized publications like franchise magazines.

Hopefully you also have the name of a contact person at the franchisor's headquarters. This individual may be the director of franchise development, franchise sales director, vice president of marketing, or even the president.

The easiest way to initiate contact with a franchisor is to send for information. Most franchising companies have tons of attractive literature because that's their first introduction to the prospect after the ad. However, franchisors also know that many who write for information aren't real prospects; thousands of folks enjoy sending for all sorts of information just for the fun of it,

and slick franchise brochures do make entertaining reading. So, franchisors who want to be friendly, polite companies, dutifully send out beautiful (and expensive) literature, knowing much of it's a waste of time and money. However, those who can't or don't wish to participate in this form of marketing will respond with a letter asking the prospect to call or visit the headquarters office.

Why doesn't the franchisor call you? In addition to the expense involved in sending out information, franchisors also discovered that the time spent making follow-up phone calls was equally nonproductive. Many times franchisors receive a hastily scribbled letter including a phone number, asking for information. They send out several dollars worth of printed material and call the prospect only to discover he or she sent out 500 other letters asking for information and doesn't even recall the franchisor or even the kind of business the franchise represents. It's for these reasons that many franchisors won't send literature through the mail or call. So don't be surprised if all you receive is a letter and perhaps an application form to test your sincerity and degree of interest.

If you're really interested in buying a particular franchise, pick up the phone and call the franchisor. Don't be afraid of being overwhelmed by a high-pressured sales pitch; as we'll discover later, the franchisor can't sell you anything or take your money until 10 business days after you've personally received a copy of the company's federal disclosure material and the franchise agreement. Using the phone works two ways: you get a feel for the company by talking to their representative, and the company gets to know you, your qualifications, and your degree of interest.

Keep in mind that companies that have been in business for five years or less are still dependent on franchise fees to cover a lot of their operating expenses. This means the sale of franchises is critical because they haven't been in business long enough for their franchisees to generate enough royalties to cover their costs. Consequently, these newer companies will try diligently to sell you a franchise and may not be as selective as other, more established organizations.

Newer franchise companies put a lot of effort into and spend a lot of money trying to sell their franchises. Their people who answer the phone and sell their franchises are experts at it. They're probably much better at selling a franchise than they are at running one. Why is this true? Most new or young franchise companies are started by entrepreneurs who are usually not only strong leaders but in many cases have a certain charisma about them that attracts strong talent. It's this powerful personality, this charisma, the prospective purchaser often faces when he or she calls for information from a new or young franchise company.

So, the newer the company, the more pressure may be put on you to buy a franchise because selling a franchise is the most important part of their business. The older and more established franchisors, although interested, normally won't exhibit the same enthusiasm or exert as much pressure as the younger company.

It's important you do your homework prior to making the call. Take the necessary time to find out how long a franchisor has been established and how many stores exist. This will give you some indication of what you're facing when you make that first call. Many potential franchisees who immediately respond to ads without doing some initial research into the organization quickly discover their ignorance puts them at the mercy of the franchisor's experienced sales staff.

When you make that first call, it's also beneficial to realize you and the franchisor may view that call as a means to two completely different ends. You're calling to get more information and hopefully to have some literature sent to you; the franchise company is using that call as a means to set up a meeting with you. Because most companies have a strong sales staff, they prefer to bring you to their office so they can use all of their people to help make the sale. If it's impossible for you to visit the company headquarters because of distance, many times the franchisor will arrange to meet you locally.

Regardless of where you meet, some franchisors will immediately mail you the Federal Trade Commission material so you have that information for the legally required 10 days prior to the meeting. In this way, less ethical franchisors can then try to "close" you at the meeting or quickly thereafter. Beware of this approach: take your time and move at your pace, not theirs.

If you're not the type to make phone calls regardless of any benefits, you *can* send a letter. However, don't write it and make a bunch of photocopies and mail them off to numerous franchisors. We tried that approach when we were gathering material for this book. We sent off 15 letters and got two responses. How come? We suspect franchisors respond to photocopied form letters the same way we do: they ignore them. It's well worth the time it takes to type each letter individually and personalize it in some way. This assures the franchisor he or she isn't merely one of a pack, all being treated the same way.

A sample letter is shown below.

                                        100 Acadia Way
                                        Machias, ME 04526
                                        March 19, 19xx

Mr. John Murchison, Vice President
Toys for Tots
500 Galivan Boulevard
San Rafael, California 93412

Dear Mr. Murchison:
    When I was visiting some friends in Boston, I had

the opportunity to talk with one of your franchisees and tour her store. She spoke highly of your organization and commented how pleased she was to be in her own business.

I am presently the marketing manager of a small toy manufacturer in Maine and want to be in my own business, preferably a retail toy store.

Would you please send me your basic franchising material? After I've had a chance to look it over, I may be back in touch with you.

Thank you in advance for your attention.

Sincerely yours,
Jane R. Johnson

Because such a letter indicates a definite interest, the franchisor may call you. Be polite and honest, but don't commit yourself to anything. Above all, don't get sold on the phone; tell the caller you are merely collecting information.

At some point mail will begin arriving, all kinds of mail. Each franchisor has a basic sales package and they're all different. Let's look at two packages from established franchisors.

ComputerLand® is a network of over 800 computer retail stores in 25 countries. The primary document in their sales kit, which they call a "Franchise Investment Portfolio," is a well-done, full-color brochure consisting of:

1. An overview of the company.
2. Market statistics.
3. Advantages of owning a store.
4. A timetable of events (including their claim it takes from 120 to 280 days to open a store from the time the franchisee is approved and his or her deposit accepted).
5. Answers to commonly asked questions.
6. Growth rate of sales since 1977.

In the back pocket of the brochure are:

1. A current list of stores, including phone numbers.
2. Square footage requirements for their three sizes of stores.
3. Estimated costs—franchise fee, fixtures, furniture and equipment, inventory, sign, real estate (purchase or rental), leasehold improvements, working capital, and start-up—and to whom these funds are paid (franchisor, suppliers, contractors).
4. A confidential application which asks for your education, employment history, references, financial statement (that's why we had you do it earlier), and some personal information.
5. A postage-paid envelope to mail in the application.

The second information packet we'll look at comes from:

Dunhill ®Personnel System, Inc., an employment agency placing professional, technical, and administrative personnel. The first Dunhill franchise was opened in 1961 and they now have over 300 offices across Canada and the United States. Their package includes:

1. A basic brochure which answers questions a potential franchisee may have—degree of training given, advantages, fees.
2. An application covering the same areas as ComputerLand's.
3. Two samples of national ads.
4. The IFA's publication, "Investigate Before Investing: Guidance for Prospective Franchisees." (A valuable booklet for all potential franchisees.)
5. A copy of their newsletter which goes to all Dunhill offices.
6. Their current training schedule.

Both of the above sales kits are informative and well-prepared, but some you receive will be neither. Again, be cautious of any material that smacks of overt salesmanship and doesn't address the kinds of questions you have—the terms of the deal, addresses of existing franchises, and so forth.

WINNOWING THE CHAFF

As you gather your data and analyze it, you'll quickly recognize there's no "right" number of franchise companies to look at. The more specific the type of business you're considering (janitorial service, for example), the fewer companies you need to contact and analyze. However, if you're looking at a lot of different companies, the next stage is to begin to focus on the most appealing ones. The best way to do this is to first eliminate those franchises that don't appeal to you for one reason or another. The most important reason for not going any further is that the business simply doesn't intrigue you. Don't ever get into a franchise just because it looks lucrative. If you get into something you don't enjoy, you'll be worse off than the majority of employed people who dislike or even hate their jobs. At least employees who don't like their jobs can quit. With your own business you can't quit; you either have to stick it out or sell it.

The next reason to reject a franchise proposal is because the cost to play the game is beyond your reach. Let's look at our previous two examples: it costs an average of $27,000 (40 percent of the $25,000 franchise fee or $10,000 plus setting-up expenses of $5,000 and 4 months' operating expenses of $12,000) to open up a Dunhill office, and an average of $390,000 to start a Computer-Land store, excluding the real estate. Even though you don't necessarily need all these funds in cash because (1) the franchisor may provide financing, (2) you may have investors who will help you, or (3) you may secure a bank loan, you can rule out those that are obviously out of reach. For example, if your total net worth is $25,000, a ComputerLand store could be eliminated from your list of potential businesses.

Here are some other initial considerations to help you trim your list:

1. Does anything about the material seem unreasonable to you? Is there a pitch telling you how rich you can be for a minimum investment? Better franchisors either totally shy away from mentioning earnings in their initial packets, or they give ranges of earnings that are documented from their experience. If the material simply looks too good to be true, that's probably just what it is.
2. Is the franchise based on either a fad or a poor business idea? Regarding fads, ask yourself whether this business will be around 10 or even 20 years from now. Many people have lost money in businesses dealing with wood stoves, solar heating, and wind turbines. Also remember that businesses may succeed in one area but not another. If you want to live in a rural area, you want to be particularly leery of businesses that rely on high traffic volume or people with cosmopolitan tastes. For example, you may be able to sell Vermont maple products in New York City, but not pâte molds in Colebrook, New Hampshire.

3. Have you been hustled in any way? It's normal for a franchisor to call you after you have their material to answer your preliminary questions, but if you feel you're being pressured, back off quickly.
4. Is this an actual, established franchise or really something else like a distributorship? Is this concept so new that, as a business, it has no track record? If it's not a true franchise or an established one, much of the security associated with owning a franchise won't be there.

AFTER THE INITIAL ANALYSIS

If you're like most folks, you've probably categorized your choices into three groups—yes, no, and maybe. How many businesses should be in the "yes" pile? Again, this depends on the individual, but five is a comfortable average. If the number gets high, say over 10, realize that it will take you more time and money to examine all these candidates properly.

The next step is to complete the application form that the franchisor has sent you. Answer the information fully and *honestly!* Lying about your background or finances will only come back on you at some later time. Before you mail the application, make a copy for yourself and file it with the other information about that franchisor.

What's the next step? You wait for the franchisor to contact you. This is done by phone or mail and you'll usually get one of three answers:

1. The franchisor wants more information. It's up to you whether you provide this or drop this group from consideration at this point.
2. Your application is rejected. The usual reason for this is financial—the franchisor feels you don't have enough capital to swing the deal. If you're turned down, you have the right to ask why. This information can be quite helpful when dealing with other franchisors.
3. Your application is approved and this information is usually relayed via a phone call. In addition to the congratulations, the caller will put some pressure on you to make the next step.

So now let's look at your next move.

CHAPTER **6**

Direct Contact

INTRODUCTION

Let's assume you've narrowed your choices to several (say between three and seven) franchisors: You're now ready to make the next step, a visit to the franchisor's headquarters. This, in fact, is exactly what the franchisor wants so you're playing into his hands when you express interest in a personal meeting. In this chapter we'll tell you what to expect so you won't feel like a fly being let loose in a den of spiders. This isn't to say that all franchisors want to do is get you on their home turf so they can snooker you and take all your money. However, they are there to sell you a franchise—that's their job; that's what pays their salaries.

Although good franchisors are concerned about their franchisee's future as well as their own, the fact remains you're responsible for looking out for your own best interests. That's why it's important for you to understand what goes on at these meetings. You don't want to get so awed by the size of the operation, its sleek executive offices, or your free room in a plush hotel that you forget the information you need to make a sound business decision.

Some franchisors are large enough to maintain regional offices in addition to national headquarters, which might mean less travel for you. This may be important, particularly if you must take time off from work to visit the facility or are on a limited budget. Regardless of where the franchisor is located, some will reimburse all or part of your traveling expenses. If this information isn't volunteered when you arrange your visit, be sure to ask. Don't be embarrassed or automatically assume the franchisor does or doesn't pay. Each company has its own policy and their employees are used to answering questions about it.

Some franchisors may come and visit you if you don't or can't come to them. Although this might seem more convenient, we strongly suggest you visit their headquarters, listen to their pitch, and ask your questions. At the very least you should talk in person with company personnel and then see either company-owned units or franchised stores.

THE VISIT ITSELF

Try to arrive the night before so you will be well rested and alert during your visit. Some companies will make a real production out of your visit to their main office; they'll meet you at the motel or airport, and give you a cook's tour of the facility plus any local units. Although the tour may look like it's an informal one, everything has been designed to impress you, the prospect. Employees of the franchisor have been coached on how to act and what part they play in the tour, so much so, one company refers to the prospect visit as a "monkey tour."

Many companies try to bring in a group of potential franchisees on a set day each month because of the beneficial effects being part of a group presentation can have on the individual. If a prospect comes in from one state and visits with others from all over the country, it's easy to get the feeling that everyone wants this franchise and then get caught up in the fervor. We're not suggesting that the deck is stacked against you under these circumstances, but group persuasion and peer pressure are certainly vital elements in any sale and something to be aware of.

Other companies hold group seminars and pull out all the stops—introducing officers of the company, showing films and slide presentations—and generally providing a pep-rally atmosphere. Companies who are still dependent on the sale of franchises for their income put on what amounts to a present-day version of the old-time medicine show. Among films, slide presentations, visits with well-dressed company officials and slick, full-color brochures, surrounded by huge maps with pins stuck all over them, it's easy for the prospect to think that he or she has found the road to instant wealth and success. Does it sound like we're exaggerating? Well, we're not. We can't overemphasize how much of a show some franchisors put on to make a sale. And although some presentations are pure Hollywood, others are deliberately understated—on purpose. Sometimes a subdued, tasteful and professional presentation can be far more effective than a medicine show when selling to certain kinds of franchisees.

So the first and foremost method franchisors use to sell the franchisee or at least create the initial interest is:

1. A presentation which can be very impressive and almost overpowering, or
2. A very professional and businesslike presentation designed to give the franchisee the feeling of "if you want to be like us, go with us."

Most franchisors provide a relatively low-key presentation, but, as we've said, some are high-pressure and others even childish. A recent public television program showed executives of a large fast-food chain that had decided to begin franchising in Japan. At critical, pre-determined times during one meeting, these managers would jump to their feet hollering, "Banzai, Banzai," evidently to unify the group. We believe the more sophomoric the presentation, the less confidence franchisor personnel have about themselves and their business. It isn't necessary to hype quality; quality speaks for itself.

In addition to formal presentations, you'll have the opportunity to talk with various individuals at headquarters—company officers, the franchise director, top salespeople. These folks are people-oriented professionals: It's this personal relationship that sells franchises and franchisors know this. However, bear in mind that many of these people (especially those with newer companies) have never run a franchise and therefore really don't understand the ins and outs of an actual franchise operation.

Also understand that most franchise salespeople work on some kind of commission; all or part of their earnings are derived from the franchises they sell. (Very good salespeople actually prefer a compensation plan based totally on commission because they're excellent "closers"; they're extremely effective at the game of selling the prospect.) And although quality salespeople realize hit-and-run tactics only work in the short term, there will be those who look on you as a source of income, nothing more.

During your visit you will also be shown all the franchisor's current training manuals. Examine these carefully because, if you sign up with this particular franchisor, these manuals (hopefully coupled with classroom instruction) will be giving you the background to operate your business. Do they seem overly slick and more like promotional material or hastily thrown together with a minimum of content? Or do they appear to be well-organized, informative, and easy to follow? Examining these materials will give you an idea of the type of franchisor you're dealing with and the quality of the training you can expect from them.

Another selling technique franchisors use might be called "dream along with me" where sales staff emphasize future programs now in the planning stages. In some cases these plans may include a dazzling array of products and services available to you at less cost if you join up now. Although the franchisor is well within legal bounds to make such statements because they could well be true, remember that only one out of every 60 products or services planned in the United States is successful; the other 59 drop by the wayside one way or another. So don't be mesmerized by visions of future plans that may not make it. Focus on what the franchise is offering *now*. What's available *now* is what you'll be using to make your living: You can't sell what you don't have.

While visiting the franchisor, you may be taken (or sent) to selected operating franchises or given the names of some franchisees to visit in your own locale. Remember: if franchisors hand-pick locations for you, those operations will be among their best, the obviously successful ones and those the franchisor feels say good things about the company. Although it's not unheard of, these franchises aren't usually being paid or rewarded by the company; however, they might expect and get special treatment when it comes to service. Therefore, these franchises can be a reliable source of information, but bear in mind you're being diverted there for a purpose.

One valuable piece of information to ask the franchisor for is the name, address, and phone number of any franchisee who *hasn't* been successful. The franchisor has no legal obligation to provide this information and therefore it may be quite difficult for you to obtain it. On the other hand, it's an interesting test to put before franchisors if for no other reason than to see how they react. Those who become defensive obviously have something to hide. How a company deals with failures or setbacks is every bit as important as how they deal with success, if not more so. Even the poorest run organization can succeed if all is going well. It's when they aren't going well that true expertise makes the difference.

You should definitely visit existing franchises as a part of your overall regimen and ask a few key questions:

1. When did you buy this franchise?
2. Why did you pick this one?
3. What was your background and experience?
4. What did you want from a franchised business? Does this one give it to you?
5. What problems did you have?
6. How big is your territory? Is it exclusive?
7. What's the one biggest complaint you have about your business?
8. How are your dealings with the franchisor?
9. Do you feel the franchise fee and royalties are fair?
10. What is your personal work schedule? Does it vary? When are you busiest?
11. What general advice can you give me?
12. Would you buy this franchise again? Why? Why not?

Visit those franchisees who failed and ask them the same questions and then compare the answers of the two groups. If those that succeeded had certain backgrounds or experience (a degree in business or marketing, experience in retail, mechanics, or food service, for example) which the failures lacked, frankly evaluate your own attributes or deficiencies in these areas. Are those who failed just trying to blame the franchisor, or is there something really lacking in the latter's training program? If those who succeeded worked 80-hour weeks and had to take crash courses at the local community college to fill gaps in the franchisor's training program, you might want to consider a different path to "success."

What if the franchisor tells you "We've never had a failure." This statement can be one of three things:

1. Totally true. If this is the case, either you're dealing with the most phenomenally successful franchise in the history of the world or it's so new no one has had the opportunity to fail yet.
2. Totally false. If you discover the franchisor is lying, back off immediately. Very few people tell only one lie—falsehoods build on one another and if the franchisor lies to you now, what do you think will happen in your later dealings?
3. Partially false. Some of the larger, more visible franchisors don't even want the hint of failure to be breathed about so if they detect an impending failure (no royalty payments made or a drastic reduction in them) they send a team of their own people in to rescue the business and turn it around. The public is usually unaware anything's happened, and "failure," i.e., the closing of the franchise, is averted. However, what was once a franchisee-owned operation may now be company-owned.

URGENT SELLING TECHNIQUES

Some franchisors try to create a sense of urgency in one of three ways to sell a franchise. The first way is to announce that the franchise fee will be increased in a short time. That "short time" might be a month but, more likely, it'll be more than a year away. To be sure, if a franchise company is growing and has a desirable product or service, chances are the fee will increase over time; but this increase is gradual. It takes time to build a franchise system into a national or international entity because too-rapid expansion usually spells doom. How can you tell whether the proclaimed fee increases are real or merely sales hype? Ask to see the history of franchise fees—if they've been increased frequently, you can assume the pattern will continue. However, if they've remained the same for quite some time, chances are any proposed hike in the near future is more likely hype.

The second method used to prod a prospect is the urgent-training-schedule routine. The franchisor tells you there's a training class beginning next week and if you don't join up now you'll have to wait until the next session is held in six months. Don't be rushed and don't allow yourself to get hustled.

The most popular way to get you moving involves the issue of territory. Suppose you're from Gary, Indiana, and you're impressed with Freddie's French-Fried Frogslegs. When the Freddie's people find this out they may pull the old routine about already having someone who's interested in Gary. This may or may not be true. If they do try this on you, simply ask, "Well, who is it?" They won't tell you even if it's true, but the question will make them aware of your knowledge of their tactics and give you an idea of how they run their business. In addition to trying to create a sense of urgency by suggesting someone else could possibly claim "your" territory, franchisors may try to lure you to sign up by offering larger areas. Obviously if they give you a protected territory that includes an entire town of 25,000 that's better than having only the southern half of that town. Franchisors will manipulate territory because it is one of the few parts of the basic franchise agreement that isn't fixed. For example, they can't readily reduce the franchise fee for you without doing it for everyone because the Federal Trade Commission (FTC) forbids that kind of behavior. However, territory can be a rather blurred issue. Contracts usually don't specify that a *specific* sized territory comes with the franchise, although many guarantee a minimum—10,000 people, one town, several counties. However, a fixed minimum doesn't mean there's a fixed maximum, so if a franchisor is interested in closing you quickly, the salesperson or franchise director may throw in the next block, the next town, the next county. This extra, added attraction is meant to give you the feeling you're getting more for your money.

QUESTIONS FOR THE FRANCHISOR

Our discussion has probably made you aware of some questions you'd like to ask the franchisor. Here's a list of 25 key questions we think the franchisor should be able to answer during your visit:

1. How much money can I make? Good franchisors will be cautious about this answer and the really good ones may even low-ball you, that is, give you an extremely conservative estimate. It's certainly better to tell you to expect an annual salary of $25,000 and have you make $40,000 than the reverse. Some franchisors will give you a range that represents what other owners have experienced in their first year. Still others relate that figure to sales, in which case it's expressed as a percent. For example, if you're told you can expect to take home 15 percent of sales as earnings, if you sell $100,000, you make $15,000; $200,000 in sales will net you $30,000 and so on.

2. When can I expect to begin making money? This is a vital question because you need to consider this factor in your financial planning. If you open a nationally known fast-food restaurant in virgin territory, you can expect to make money the first month or at least the second. If you open a service business or a retail business offering a new concept or product, it may take a year to build up sufficient clients or customers to turn a profit. For example, a franchise selling New England clam chowder may take less time to become established on Cape Cod than one selling California tacos. Franchised tutorial services may have to overcome parental reluctance

to use them or provide proof of their merit before they can generate enough business to provide an income for their owners.

3. How much money must I personally invest? What does this include? How much is working capital?

4. Do you do any financing? If not, will you help me to secure it? NOTE: The majority of franchisors do neither, but you always ask because you might be dealing with the exception.

5. How many franchised locations do you have? How many are company-owned? How many of each have failed? Why did they fail?

6. What happens if I'm not successful due to my efforts? Suppose it's your fault—introducing products that don't sell, or picking the wrong location?

7. Is there any way you'll buy me back? Can either of us initiate this?

8. When do I pay you? This is important because some franchisors will allow you to stretch out the franchise fee. You also want to know how often you pay royalties.

9. How long is the process from contract signing to opening day?

10. Is the business seasonal? What affects business levels? One fast-food restaurant found their sales increased in recessionary periods. Some retail establishments experience their biggest rush during the Christmas season whereas those geared to tourist products and services may do the majority of their business in one particular season.

11. What is the nature of your training support? How long does it last? What will I learn? May I see the manuals?

12. What am I required to buy from you? Do I have to buy a minimum amount? What is your markup on what you sell to me?

13. What staff support can I count on? The larger, more established franchisors have internal consultants available and if this is the case, ask if you have to pay for their services.

14. What advertising and promotion do you do? Am I expected to do a certain amount of local advertising? Are there advertising payments to you based on my sales?

15. Who will be my contact? What happens if that person leaves?

16. What are your plans for the next five years?

17. What makes you think this business will succeed in my area?

18. What are my hours of operation? Must I work full-time at the business? Can I start in my house?

19. What exactly is my territory?

20. Do I own the equipment?

21. Do you find the location for me? Who owns the real estate?

22. Do you have a newsletter?

23. What seminars and courses do you hold for present franchisees?

24. What exclusive rights do I have? Can I sell the business myself?

25. May I see a contract now? How long is the contract good for? Is it renewable? How can I terminate it? How can you? What happens if I die?

We could go on, but this gives you the basic idea of the kinds of information you should obtain during your visit.

BRINGING THE MEETING TO AN END

Before you leave, the franchisor may tell you they'll get back to you if you've qualified for the franchise. This qualification in many cases isn't really an actual process but rather just a ruse to let you think you're being evaluated.

Many companies will also ask you to sign a letter of intent, a letter of interest or some other document. Such a letter isn't legally binding, but it does begin the process of getting you involved and is one more step toward the successful sale of a franchise. It also gives the salespeople who follow up your visit more confidence when they contact you again because you've indicated a degree of interest.

Once you leave the franchisor's headquarters, the barrage begins. If the franchising company decides you're interested, you'll be inundated by all kinds of communication with the staff. If you've shown an urgency to buy, are looking for your own business, and aren't presently employed (and therefore could sign and begin immediately) you'll be number 1 on the franchisor's list. Don't be hustled or hurried: Do it at your own pace. Once you're home again, take time to reflect on what you've learned and answer the questions below. If any of your answers make you nervous, back out of the deal *now*. Don't prolong the agony.

1. Is this franchise so new they have no track record and therefore are really selling promises rather than performance?
2. Was I pressured in any way?
3. Did the contract seem vague?
4. Did the franchisor's presentation or material smack of a get-rich-quick scheme?
5. Were the people I met the kind I'd like to be in business with?
6. Are there heavy initial fees that can't be justified by the operation of the business?
7. Were all my questions answered willingly and to my satisfaction?
8. Did the company give me references?
9. Was I told this was my last chance to sign up and, if not, the deal was off?
10. Was I discouraged from having professionals—attorneys, accountants, consultants—look over the deal?

After the hope and excitement of your visit, you may find yourself feeling a bit confused as you try to sort through those piles of materials in your own home. In the next chapter we'll take a look at the legal obligations of franchisor and franchisee to help you sort out the meaningful information from the slick presentation and promotional hype.

CHAPTER 7

Your Legal Rights: Federal Trade Commission Disclosure

INTRODUCTION

We've already alluded to the Federal Trade Commission (FTC) and their Franchise Rule which is formally called the "Disclosure Requirements and Prohibitions Concerning Franchising and Business Opportunity Ventures." The information that a franchisor must supply you in accord with these regulations is often referred to as the "disclosure document" or sometimes just "the FTC material," or "The Rule." In this chapter we'll be going into "The Rule" in some detail but only to the extent that it affects you and your prospective new business. If, for some reason, you want to read The Rule in its entirety, you can look it up in the *Federal Register,* Vol. 44, No. 166, of Friday, August 24, 1979, pp. 49966–49992, or write to the FTC, 6th and Pennsylvania Avenue, NW, Washington, DC 20580, for a copy.

Before a franchisor can legally take your money or get you to sign a binding agreement, the company must give you their FTC disclosure as well as a copy of the agreement or contract they want you to sign. And they must furnish you this material ten business days before you fork over any dough or sign that document. As a matter of fact, you *can't* sign the agreement for five business days after you've received it. There-

fore, we're going to go over this legal material just as you should be doing in that ten-day interval. However, we're going to take the legal-sounding phraseology out and tell you in plain language what the FTC requires, what this information can do for you and, more importantly, what it doesn't do for you. Also be aware that about half the states in the United States have what's known as "baby FTC acts"; the states usually followed the FTC's lead and copied most of what the federal agency did and added a few wrinkles of their own. Other countries— Canada, the United Kingdom, Japan—have also enacted similar laws, so make sure any franchise you're considering meets the requirements of any local or international regulations that may come into play in that type of business.

THE ROLE OF THE FTC AND YOU

The first and the most important feature to recognize is that the FTC cannot (and will not) certify the information you receive. It's up to you to investigate what the franchisor says. It's important to be aware of this because many government agencies can and do regulate what you receive. When you buy USDA Choice meat you know it's been graded and inspected by a qualified representative of the Department of Agriculture. The fact that a franchisor must give you a copy of the FTC regulations is no guarantee that the company is in compliance with those regulations. However, even though there are few teeth in the law, in most cases it works. The better franchisors obey the spirit and intent of The Rule simply because they want to do business the right way. Others comply out of fear, but whether or not that fear is well grounded depends on your point of view. To be sure, the FTC can seek civil penalties of up to $10,000 for each violation of The Rule as well as an injunction (a court ruling to make the company stop what they're doing) against any continuing violations. However, it's not done very often; as you might well expect, it takes an effort on the part of dissatisfied franchisees to get a suit into federal court and then, when all the legal posturing is over, to prevail in that suit. In most cases the cost of such a suit in time and money is sufficiently beyond the means of even a group of small franchisees and few opt to pursue their "legal" rights.

To cite the FTC's own language, "Although the FTC cannot act directly to resolve your problem, the staff is interested in gathering information on the subject." In other words, the FTC can't help you select a reputable franchisor but if you get into trouble, they'd like to know about it. If the FTC can't help you check out a franchisor, what can you do yourself? Here are some suggestions:

1. Have your accountant analyze the franchisor's latest annual report. Copies of this may be on file at large university or public libraries. Or you can request a copy from the company's treasurer. There will also be some financial information in the franchisor's disclosure material.
2. If the company is privately held and therefore has no annual report, contact the local office of Dun & Bradstreet; for a fee they'll provide reports on businesses.
3. Contact your state attorney general's office to see if there is anything negative on file regarding the franchisor—complaints, lawsuits.
4. Find towns in which the franchisor has locations and check with local Better Business Bureaus and Chambers of Commerce.

5. Write to the Council of Better Business Bureaus, Inc., 1150 17th Street, NW, Washington, DC 20036, as well as the FTC's Bureau of Consumer Affairs (address on page 45). However, remember these agencies can only tell you if *they've* received negative information. Just because they haven't received any doesn't necessarily mean there isn't any.
6. Visit a large public library and examine the microfilm indexes of past issues of the *Wall Street Journal* and *The New York Times* for the past 2 to 3 years. Check under the franchisor's name and under the heading "Franchising." Read any article that might be directly or indirectly related to the company you're considering. Also consult *Reader's Guide to Periodic Literature* and the *Business Periodicals Index* for other articles.

REGULATION OF FRANCHISES

Since the early 1970s, many states have enacted laws regulating the offering and subsequent sale of franchises. Therefore, there are now many state laws in effect in addition to The Rule set down in 1979 by the FTC. However, until the tail end of 1978 a franchisor could do exactly what Plants-For-Everyone did to Mary Knolls and get away with it. And even with The Rule in effect, some franchisors still manage to pull the same scam.

What exactly does the FTC ruling say? The Rule basically states that certain information about the franchisor must be disclosed in writing to a prospective franchisee. And, as we've noted, the franchisor can't accept money or ask you to sign a binding agreement until 10 days after you've received this information; remember, this information must also include a copy of the franchise agreement (contract) that they want *you* to sign. However, The Rule goes a step further—it states the disclosure material must be presented to you at the first *personal* meeting. So even if a franchisor mails you this material, the ten-day clock doesn't start ticking—legally anyway—until you meet face to face.

We need to make a side comment here about required time periods, because it can get confusing. There is really both a ten-day and a five-day requirement. The Rule states that a franchisor must provide you with the FTC disclosure material and a *sample* (not actual) contract 10 days in advance of your signing anything. The five days refers to the waiting period for your specific contract. Suppose, then, a franchisor gives you the required material and *your* agreement on the same day. Do you have to wait 10 days or five? You must wait the full 10 business days. On the other hand, let's assume you got the FTC material and a sample contract but nothing else for 10 business days. On the 11th day you receive your agreement. Can you sign it then? No, you must now wait five additional business days.

When we refer to the five-day period, keep in mind it refers to the interval between receiving an actual contract and its signing by you.

The time restrictions of the process and cost of printing the material has also created problems for franchisors. On the one hand they want prospective buyers to have the disclosure material as soon as feasible so they can legally close a deal as quickly as possible. On the other, large franchisors get many, many people passing through and indiscriminately handing out that "pound of paper," as they often call the disclosure material, can get expensive. Consequently, you may run into franchisors who may actually be a bit hesitant about handing out this information. In general most franchisors use one of two approaches. They mail you the disclosure material and then begin the ten-day hustle when you meet. Or, the franchisor may be reluctant to give you that data until they're certain you're (1) qualified and (2) interested. Question: Which approach do you feel better with?

In the opinion of most franchise experts, the "first personal meeting" that starts the ten-day clock occurs when you and a representative of the franchisor discuss details of the franchise on a one-to-one basis. At this time most franchisors will ask you to sign a receipt for the documents. This protects them from disgruntled franchisees who come along later demanding their money back, claiming they never received the required documentation, or didn't have it for the required length of time.

Let's take a closer look at what's contained in the FTC disclosure material. We're not going to quote a bunch of legal stuff but it's important for you to know what you'll be receiving and how to interpret what you read. You may want to take any documents you receive to your lawyer. If you do this, be careful. Some lawyers:

1. Tend to nit-pick and worry over insignificant terms and phrases. Even if an attorney finds something that doesn't seem right to him or her, your chances of getting a franchisor to change it are slim. For one thing, they'll use the FTC rule to say they can't change. The FTC specifically states that whatever a franchisor does for one franchisee, it must do for all. Thus, when you ask them to change something for you, by law they must change it for everyone. What you must decide is whether any discrepancy you find is sufficient to cause you to back out of the deal. If it's discovered that the franchisor has made an error in the age of the chief executive officer, that's a small matter compared to failing to reveal that the CEO was indicted on fraud charges.

2. Like many other professionals, are now actively engaged in methods to increase their income. Without some check on the time they spend (which can cost you $50 to $150 per hour), they can easily eat up funds you'll need for getting into business.

3. Know little about business. Be a tad careful about accepting advice from an attorney whether or not your choice of a particular franchise is a good *business* idea. Keep them within their own field—determining whether the documents presented by the franchisor are in order.

THE FTC DISCLOSURE MATERIAL

In essence the FTC's rules say you have the right to:

1. Not be misled orally or in writing by anything inconsistent with the requirements of The Rule. Remember the line from the *Wizard of Oz* when Toto, Dorothy's little dog, exposed the Wizard? "Pay no attention to that man behind the curtain." If you get that approach—"Pay no attention to the legal stuff. What we really do is . . . ."—back off.

2. Receive substantiation for any earnings assumptions. If a franchisor says you can make $100,000 a year, you can ask how that figure was derived. It should come from actual case histories, not some projection based on what they think will happen.

3. Have the documentation, FTC disclosure material and sample agreement, in your possession for at least 10 days. This means the franchisor can't force you to sign an agreement in less than 10

days, nor can they change an offer during this time. Once you receive the *actual* contract, you must hold it for five business days before you sign.

4. Receive any refunds that are promised by the franchisor in accordance with any limitations set down. For example, if the franchisor's material states, "All monies will be refunded within 30 days of signing the agreement if you're not totally satisfied," then all you need to do is say you're not totally satisfied and you will receive your money back.

The Rule requires franchisors to provide information on 20 subjects. When you look at a particular franchisor's disclosure material, you may not see exactly 20 sections; you may see more or less depending on how the franchisor assembles the information. What's important is whether or not all the bases have been covered.

1. *Identifying information about the franchisor.* This may be brief and simple covering company address, year of incorporation, number of employees, names of affiliates, names of any predecessor companies.

2. *Business experience of the franchisor's directors and key executives.* Remember that members of a board of directors, although legally charged with representing the stockholders' (owners') interests, may meet only a few times a year, so sterling credentials may have little effect on the day-to-day operations of the company. However, be leery if acknowledged experience seems to have little relevancy to the company's stated purpose and goals. Although two rock stars, an Olympic skier, and TV's favorite courtroom judge may add glamour to the board meetings, the chances of their providing much guidance to the Easy Lawn Care Specialist Company is doubtful. Also, scan the list for nepotism; spouses, children, and in-laws of the CEO often have different goals than more objective, unrelated business associates.

3. *The franchisor's business experience.* There are two things to look at here and both pertain to history. First, look back at (2) above and then compare the length of time executives have been

with the company versus the number of years the franchisor has been in business. Second, take note of whether the company was in business for a while but is new to franchising. The best bet overall is a company with a successful track record as a franchisor (five years or more) and officers who've been with the company a reasonable length of time (at least two years).

4. *Litigation history of the franchisor and its directors and key executives.* Like (3.) above, the key phrase you're looking for here is, "Neither the franchisor, nor any person heretofore mentioned, is or has been subject to . . . blah, blah, blah . . . legal phrases . . . etc." You're looking for clean slates.

6. *Description of the franchise.* This section may not appear, *per se,* if enough data has been provided in (1.) and (3.) above. If it does appear, it will be in relatively simple terms. "Franchisor is engaged in the sale of franchises which sell lingerie and intimate apparel for women."

7. *Money required to be paid by the franchisee to obtain or commence the franchise operation.* This refers to the franchise fee, and may be headed "Franchisee's Initial Franchise Fee." It states the total dollar amount and how it's to be paid—all at once, spread over some number of months. Often there's a clause about refunding the initial franchise fee, under what conditions it's possible, and any deductions that the franchisor will make from that fee. For example, the disclosure material may state that you can have a refund up until the time you finish your training, but the franchisor may subtract the cost of training from that refund.

8. *Continuing expenses to the franchisee in operating the franchise business that are payable in whole or in part to the franchisor.* Please note that this part of The Rule only talks about monies paid to the franchisor; these costs can include royalties, equipment, supplies. Naturally, you'll have start-up expenses—insurance, furniture, printing, fidelity bond, tax deposits, rent and utility deposits,

leasehold improvements—that will be paid to other parties. You'll also need working capital to keep the business going until you're profitable. Third, you need to consider your own living expenses. Many franchisors will provide you with estimates of start-up and working capital but only you can work out what you need to live on. If the franchisor gives you a range of expenses, use the higher values to be safe. Otherwise, take the numbers provided and increase them 50 to 100 percent; this should give you the needed safety margin. Definitely double the amount of working capital needed. This will double the amount of time it'll take you to be profitable: as the old saying goes, it's better to be safe than sorry. The important thing to keep in mind is that the disclosure of continuing expenses required by the FTC are only those payable to the franchisor; and those expenses are only part of the expenses you will have. Whether or not the franchisor gives you additional estimates is a matter of choice; and you are solely responsible for the evaluation of this material as it pertains to you and your lifestyle.

9. *A list of persons who are either the franchisor or any of its affiliates, with whom the franchisee is required or advised to do business.* In the early days of franchising, franchisors used the franchise agreement to force franchisees to purchase goods, supplies, and materials from them. The reasoning was sound because franchising was conceived as a means of distributing goods and products more effectively and efficiently. If you had the Singer sewing machine franchise, you were supposed to sell Singer sewing machines—not someone else's sewing machines. But as the years went on, franchisors began making their franchisees buy everything from them and many times at a much higher price—sort of a new version of the "company store." A few years ago the courts ruled against these so-called "tying arrangements," where the franchisee is "tied" to the franchisor in such a way that the franchisor completely controls the franchisee. However, franchisors still have the right, as they should, to insure that the quality of goods and products used and/or sold by the franchisee meet the franchisor's quality standards. So, as a franchisee, you have the right to purchase goods and supplies from other suppliers if the franchisor

has approved either the supplier or the quality of the goods—or both. Remember, part of a successful franchise system is consistent quality, not just cost efficiency. Without that consistency, franchising doesn't work and probably doesn't have a basis for existence. If the reason customers continually seek out Sanitary Maintenance Systems is because of their high-quality paper products, they can't afford to let a franchisee save a few dollars by buying inferior goods. Consequently, franchisors normally have the right to make you buy from them certain key ingredients that make their product or service unique to the marketplace.

10. *Realty, personalty, services, and so forth, which the franchisee is required to purchase, lease, or rent, and a list of any persons from whom such transactions must be made.* This section may be tied with (8.) above. You have the right to know where else you must purchase equipment, supplies, and inventory if not from the franchisor. Because of court intervention in the matter of tying arrangements, many franchisors list what is required, a sign, for example, and then designate the source merely as "third party," which means you can go where you please for your sign. However, that sign will have to meet franchisor specifications.

11. *Description of consideration paid (such as royalties, commissions, and so forth) by third parties to the franchisor or any of its affiliates as a result of a franchisee's purchase from such third parties.* Simply stated this means that the franchisor has to disclose "kickback" schemes. Going back to the matter of the sign, let's suppose that Wally's Worldwide Burgers signs an agreement with the Gross Day-Glo Sign Co., that all franchisees must buy their signs there. Although there will be a fixed price for the sign, say $3,000, Wally's gets a 5 percent "royalty" ($150) every time a franchisee buys a sign from Gross. Wally's must tell you this is the case.

12. *Description of any franchisor assistance in financing the purchase of a franchise.* As we said earlier, few franchisors do any financing. A small percentage will finance the franchise fee and/or

other expenses. Another minority will assist you in finding financing, but you should count on securing conventional financing, most normally a commercial bank loan. (We'll touch on bank dealings in Chapter 11.) There are two other items that you may see in this section: (a) the intent or lack of it to discount notes or contracts to a third party (what Plants-For-Everyone did with Mary Knoll's $5,000 note) and (b) the receipt of payments received by the franchisor for placing financing with a particular institution. This latter provision is called a placement fee but, in reality, is just a form of kickback.

13. *Restrictions placed on a franchisee's conduct of its own business.* The language in this section is quite strong; the words used are: will, shall, must, be required to, is obligated for. This list of don'ts varies greatly from one franchisor to another. We won't go into detail here because the list could contain almost anything you could imagine; but be sure to read this part carefully. One item to pay strict attention to is the opening of your own business(es) in competition with the franchisor. Remember the Jitney-Jungle story in Chapter 1? The owner of all those competing businesses might be mad, but he did violate the contract and, as the court held, therefore owed royalties on those outlets he started. Another restriction might be territory and the fact that you can't operate outside a certain geographic area. Be advised, though, that the courts haven't looked kindly on exclusivity and restriction because they see it as being "in restraint of trade," a favorite phrase of the FTC. Still, any kind of litigation is time-consuming and expensive. If you're not comfortable with the restrictions, don't get involved with the franchise.

14. *Required personal participation by the franchisee.* This may also be tied in with (13.). One franchisor states that franchisees are "obligated to work full time and use best efforts [whatever that means] in the promotion and building of the business. Franchisee is prohibited in actively engaging in *any other business* [emphasis ours], whether as a principal, agent, employee, partner or otherwise during the term of the franchise

agreement." So, under that agreement, you must spend all your efforts on that business and can't do anything else. What if you're the kind of person who wants to do several things at once and are capable of carrying it off? How do you feel about this kind of limitation?

15. *Termination, cancellation, and renewal of franchise.* This section usually spells out in great detail how you can renew, cancel, assign (to a new owner) your franchise agreement and your business. It will also spell out in very great detail how and why the franchisor can terminate your franchise agreement. It's very important that you read and understand these provisions, even though they're exceedingly dull. However, your failure to understand how you can lose your franchise can come back to haunt you in the future. For example, most franchise agreements are for a specified period of time; at the end of that period you can renew the agreement for a specified fee (usually more than the initial fee) and by signing the franchise agreement currently in use. It is this latter stipulation that can change things dramatically. Franchisors change their agreements as the company matures; royalties, advertising and other fees can go up. When your agreement ends, that new franchise agreement you will be asked to sign could contain these higher fees and other conditions not in your original agreement. On the other hand, if the franchise company has become bigger and stronger, the benefits of continuing your relationship with the franchisor may be well worth the increased fees.

16. *Statistical information about the number of franchises and their rate of terminations.* Note the use of the word "statistical." This means that under The Rule a franchisor doesn't have to give you names, only numbers. Look very carefully at the numbers: if the franchisor is a mature company, you should see a 5 to 15 percent failure rate because even the best franchisors have franchisee failures. If there are no failures listed and it's not a new franchise, be careful: very little in our world is 100 percent.

17. *Franchisor's right to select or approve a site for the franchise.* Most franchisors reserve this right; they simply don't want you operating out of a location that will lower the image of their business. The franchisor may also reserve the right to send people to analyze your proposed location for business potential. It's been said many times that in retail there are only three things that are important: location, location, and location.

18. *Training programs for the franchisee.* Beware of any franchisor who leaves this blank. Most franchisors do provide training, ranging from a day or two for simple, small businesses to up to a month for more complex ones. Be certain you understand what is provided. Remember the business skills inventory you did earlier? If there are gaps in your business knowledge, see if the franchisor will be covering those areas in the training.

19. *Celebrity involvement with the franchise.* This section of the FTC disclosure goes back to the days of Minnie Pearl Fried Chicken. Famous athletes and entertainers loaned their names to franchise companies whose owners hoped people would not only patronize these businesses, but just as importantly, consider buying a franchise because of the prestige of associating with the "public" figures. Most of these companies failed, taking many millions of dollars and lots of broken dreams with them. Public figures don't make successful franchises; sound concepts, training, and support, when coupled with diligent franchisees, do.

20. *Financial information about the franchisor.* This data is often given in the form of an annual report—balance sheet and income statement—for the past business year. You may want your accountant to go over this if you're not comfortable with the numbers. These financial statements are usually audited by outside accounting firms, and give the financial strength of the franchisor. If the franchisor has no money and is also losing money from the franchise operations, their ability to supply training and support may be hampered by the lack of funds. On the other hand, lots of available cash on the balance sheet doesn't necessarily mean that the franchisor is willing to spend it to furnish support—it could mean that they have all this cash because they haven't supplied all the support they should have. Again, the best measure of the franchisor is the success of their franchisees.

These 20 areas must be covered in a single document, but the franchisor can include other information as long as it's consistent with the required data. Some of this other information might include:

1. Obligations of the franchisor. This usually contains a rather interesting selection of words. You may remember we said under section (13.) of The Rule that words like "shall" and "must" are used to describe your activities. Well, when it comes to the franchisor's obligations, we're more likely to see phrases such as "from time to time," "upon request," "best efforts basis," and "at its sole discretion."

2. Trademarks, copyrights, registered names. This section points out all of the mentioned items owned by the franchisor and spells out your rights, if any, to them. If you're dealing with a fairly new franchise, it's important to contact the state in which you are going to do business to see if the franchisor has registered the name. You don't want to go to register the name of the franchisor, which may be an important part of what you're buying, only to find that someone else is using a name close enough to your new name and you're prohibited from using it. Even large franchisors have run into this problem. There are stories where even McDonald's found a problem going into new marketplaces where someone else named McDonald had a hamburger stand and had registered its name prior to the time Ray Kroc began selling franchises.

Other sections of the disclosure must tell you how you must report income to the franchisor and how the franchisor can check on you. Read this carefully; it may say that if the franchisor "suspects" that you're not reporting properly, they can send in an audit team to check out your financial statements, books and records. And this can be at your expense, even if you filed correctly. Sometimes if you didn't "properly" report a percentage of sales, it could mean that you must pay that amount plus the total audit bill. Make sure you understand how and when the franchisor expects you to pay the royalty and other fees.

Again, the important thing to remember about The Rule is that it only stipulates four specific rights for you as a franchisee:

- Not to be misled orally or in writing by anything inconsistent with the requirements of The Rule.
- To receive substantiation for any earnings assumptions.
- To have the documentation, FTC disclosure material, and sample agreement for no less than 10 days and your specific contract for five business days.
- To receive any refunds that are promised by the franchisor in accordance with any limits set down.

Beyond that, The Rule simply requires that the franchisor offers you information in 20 areas. However, it does not evaluate this information. The fact that a franchisor complies with FTC regulations isn't the same as getting a USDA Choice piece of beef; it's the equivalent of getting a list of USDA guidelines and a slab of meat to grade yourself.

Although the 20 areas covered by the FTC rule may seem to cover everything, there are other aspects of your relationship with the franchisor that may only appear in the agreement. In the next chapter we'll take a look at what this legal document does and doesn't cover.

CHAPTER 8

Your Legal Rights: The Franchise Agreement

GENERAL INFORMATION

As we've said, you have a right to see a copy of the franchise agreement that you'll be asked (begged, cajoled, even bullied) to sign beforehand. Remember, once you sign it, you're legally bound to live up to the conditions of that contract; and it *is* a legally binding contract even though the word agreement is used.

Although technically the franchisor only has to furnish a copy of the agreement they want you to sign five days prior to your signing it, they usually furnish the agreement along with the FTC disclosure material 10 days beforehand.

Because the agreement is a legal contract, it should contain the five elements we covered earlier:

1. An offer. The franchisor offers to let you use its name, trademarks, processes, products.
2. An acceptance. You accept the franchisor's offer by signing the agreement. Be aware that only a limited number of contracts *must* be in writing. A court once held that a nod of the head was enough to be called acceptance.
3. Consideration. In your case, this means money.
4. Competency. You and the franchisor must be *legally* competent. Neither of you can be drunk, stoned, or insane. You must also be of legal age, usually 21.
5. Legal purchase. A franchise contract for a business that sells hand grenades wouldn't hold up in court because it's not a legal endeavor.

THE AGREEMENT ITSELF

There are no legal requirements relative to a franchise contract except that it can't be inconsistent with the disclosure material. Chances are you'll see information repeated in the agreement that's also in the FTC-required document. Remember that the agreement is legally binding and when you sign your name, you're saying you'll do what's required. Be absolutely certain you understand it all *and* are willing to abide by both the spirit and intent of what's there. For example, consider the following quote from an actual agreement:

"It is further recognized and acknowledged that advertising, while making it easier for the marketing staff to acquire new clients, will not be a self-liquidating expenditure in that initial client acquisition during said start-up period will not produce enough revenue to cover the immediate cost of said advertising. The franchise business will therefore require an initial capital investment on the part of the Franchisee."

Pretty hard to understand what they're saying, but it does appear you'd have to cough up more money initially for advertising. The question becomes how much? Find out *before* you sign.

It's important to read over the contract in detail because in addition to items that may be objectionable and distasteful to you, you may find policies that may not be applicable to your locale. We watched a fast-food restaurant in a rural town introduce breakfast omelets at nearly $4.00 a crack (no pun intended). This town is heavily blue-collar and although that group contains more breakfast-goers than their white-collar counterparts, they go for the $1.35 version of eggs and toast. Omelets, particularly expensive omelets, are reserved for special occasions.

Should you attempt contract negotiation with the franchisor? If you're dealing with a large, well-established company you can try, but you probably won't get anywhere. The big franchisors have waiting lists, so the next guy's money is as good as yours. A small, new franchisor, hungry for franchising fees and increased locations, may negotiate anything. They have to be very careful, however, not to violate the law that says if they do something for one franchisee they must do it for all. Many will simply state, "We can't change it because the government (the FTC) won't let us," and let it go.

If something bothers you, by all means bring it up. However, don't be like those people who feel they must bargain to get a good deal. You're not buying a used car. Good franchisors will listen to you because you know more about your locale than they do. For example, if the agreement requires your operation be open from 7 A.M. to 6 P.M. and your town is a "late night crowd," it might be a good idea to discuss this. Often what makes it in Dubuque might fail in Manhattan because of easily altered restrictions.

However, most franchisors won't negotiate changes in the essential part of their operation. For example, suppose you have a background in auto mechanics and are considering one of the franchised muffler-and-shock operations. The franchisor states that tailpipes must be bought from only three sources, all of which you recognize as being very expensive. You'd like to be able to go to cheaper sources, but because the franchisor has had a good history with the three suppliers—high quality, long life, rapid delivery—they don't want to change. A change could result in a lesser product, which could eventually affect customer service and eventually sales. Of course, they could also be receiving kickbacks from these suppliers and might even own one of them under a different corporate name. If the latter is the case, they should tell you this in the disclosure document. Otherwise assume the company is sticking with what has worked best for them over the widest range in the past. Although perhaps you individually could do a more efficient and effective job with product B, if product A produces more uniform results among all franchisees, that's probably what the company will use. The issue here isn't what they use so much as how much it bothers you.

WHAT'S IN AN AGREEMENT?

Let's go over a typical agreement. Again we'll stay away from the legal jargon and present the sections in the order they might occur in an actual case.

1. *Parties.* This is that "party of the first part" stuff. It simply names you and the franchisor.
2. *Recitals.* This section typically has anywhere from 2 to 20 "whereas's." A typical sentence might read, "WHEREAS, Franchisor has established a reputation as a specialized type of business entity with unique and proprietary methods, processes, techniques, applications, and capabilities that have proved of benefit . . . ." and so forth. In essence it describes those events and/or qualities of you and the franchisor that led up to the two of you signing this agreement. Unfortunately, the way most are written, if you didn't know the circumstances beforehand, it's doubtful the recital will enlighten you much.
3. *Grant of Franchise.* This very brief section says that the franchisor is willing to license the franchise.
4. *Term and Renewal.* Most agreements run for a

specific time, often five years. After that they must be renewed. This is done by writing to the franchisor, usually 90 days before the agreement runs out. But here's the kicker—you'll have to abide by the "terms and conditions as are contained in new franchise agreements then in effect by Franchisor." In other words, you'll have to kick in *another* franchise fee, and it'll most likely be higher than what you paid before! Furthermore, any changes (new suppliers, services, or restrictions) will also come into effect at that time. For example, in the 17 years Jack Horvath has owned his auto supply franchise he's paid franchise fees four times: when he initially started his business and at renewal years 5, 10, and 15. At year 10 Jack lost the right to handle his own advertising and had to submit all ad copy to the franchisor from that time on. His renewal two years ago gave him access to the franchisor's new computerized accounting system. Get in touch with current franchisees to discover what kinds of changes have been made in the past. If you're dealing with a new franchisor, be aware that the life expectancy of your business as described in that contract is not guaranteed beyond its termination date. Without any past record to go on you have no idea what changes could occur.

5. *Location*. Most franchisors want some say about where you're going to operate the business and many will either specify the building or office, or, at the very least, retain the right to approve or reject any location you select.

6. *Fees*. As already mentioned, the franchisor must spell out in detail the various fees that are required, when they're due, and what they're for.

7. *Obligations of the Franchisor and Franchisee*. These two sections are probably the longest and may be exact copies of what's in the disclosure material. Read them *very carefully*. If you sign this document, you will be legally bound by what it says. Remember what we said before—observe carefully for your obligations couched in terms like "shall," "must," "will refrain from," "will be required to maintain, to pay, and to do" versus a franchisor bound only by "might's" and "maybe's." One of a franchisor's favorite clauses sometimes appearing after all its obligations, is "Franchisee does hereby agree to indemnify Franchisor against any liabilities arising from any failure on the part of the Franchisor to perform the duties and obligations herein mentioned and to hold Franchisor harmless

therefrom." If you agree to "indemnify and hold harmless" the franchisor, you're saying you won't blame them or sue them if they fail to do the things they promise. If such a clause appears in the contract you may want to look for a similar one that indemnifies and holds you harmless, too. If you don't find one, carefully evaluate how you feel: does this bother you? Or does it seem all right? If it bothers you, it's bound to affect your working relationship with these people.

8. *Pricing Structure*. The franchisor can take one of three routes:
   (a) They can set the prices you must charge. This could either help or hurt you: people in New York City are used to paying twice as much for a hot dog as folks in rural Montana. A Montana Dog franchise selling 75¢ hot dogs in Manhattan might be a huge success as the lunch crowd's bargain of the century. A Big Apple Dogs, Inc. franchise selling $2.50 hot dogs in Sandy Creek, Montana, might not fare so well. Also, such an approach may not be legal, coming under the category of price fixing;
   (b) They can give you a suggested retail price list, or;
   (c) They can allow you to charge what you want.

The second option is probably best—you're given guidelines but aren't locked into them.

9. *Advertising*. This part of the agreement may cover such areas as:
   (a) what fees, if any, you're required to pay for national or local, co-operative advertising.
   (b) the freedoms and restrictions on your own advertising. This varies greatly from one franchisor to another. Generally you can advertise locally, but you'll probably have to submit your ad copy to the franchisor for approval. In no case we know are you able to change things like trademarks, slogans, logos, trade names, and the like.

10. *Hiring People*. You're normally free to hire who you want because you'll be paying their wages or commissions; but you may be required to follow certain procedures—having them complete a company application form, sign an employment agreement, provide a bond, or even take a lie detector test. One franchisor requires employees obtain a certificate of automobile insurance for a job that doesn't require the individual to have a car. In this section the franchisor may state that you are an independent business-

person and not an employee of the franchise company.

11. *Recordkeeping and Reporting Requirements.* As the title implies, here the franchisor tells you how to keep your business records and for how long. Because continuing fees are a normal part of the franchisor-franchisee arrangement, you're told when to send money; it's usually every 30 days. The franchisor will also state that they can come and examine those records, often with *no advance warning.* If a franchisor says they can conduct surprise inspections (and even charge you for them), what does that say to you about how that franchisor views its franchisees? Again, at issue here isn't so much whether what they do is right or wrong, but how you feel about it.

12. *Territory.* Exclusive territories are rare if for no other reason than they might be illegal. On the other hand, you'll probably be restricted to a certain town or a portion of it. Does this mean a franchisor can license someone else to set up shop across the street from you? Yes it does, but most franchisors won't do this because their royalty income would suffer, to say nothing of the negative effect of the ill-will created between the two franchisees battling for the same market.

13. *Termination of Franchise and Procedure Upon Termination.* This is an interesting section and should be read very carefully. The causes for termination are pretty one-sided: You can get bounced out for some things you'd expect (abandoning the business, not paying the fees when you're supposed to, outright deceit), and some things you may not expect (failure to complete prescribed training programs, spending a night in jail, and a real fuzzy one like "anything which negatively affects the franchise operation"). Whereas the franchisor may have a long list of causes to terminate their relationship with you, you may have only one—"material default"—to terminate your relationship with them. Terminating by virtue of their material default requires you prove they didn't do what they said they'd do. If you agreed, back in section (7.), not to hold the franchisor responsible for the failure to perform their duties and obligations, or accepted their obligations in the form of "might do this" or "may do that," you may find yourself with little legal ground to stand on if the franchisor reneges on any portion of such a nebulously defined agreement. This section also spells out the actual procedures that take place in a termination. You'll have to give

back anything that belongs to the franchisor, stop doing business, and may have to pay a termination fee.

14. *Limitations of Franchisee.* This is a list of "you can'ts." For example, an agreement may state that you can't:
   a. Sell the franchise without the franchisor's approval of the new owner.
   b. Alter anything—logos, uniforms, methods.
   c. Buy from suppliers not approved by franchisor.
   d. Work at *any* other business.
   e. Get any but their designated insurance coverage.
   f. Divulge trade secrets.
   g. Use the equipment and supplies of your business for anything else.
   h. Bad-mouth the franchisor.
   i. Assign any of your rights to another person.
   The list could be quite long. Interestingly, you probably won't find anything entitled "Limitations of Franchisor."

15. *Miscellaneous Clauses.* Most of these are standard to most contracts and include:
   a. *Applicable Law.* The franchisor must select a state whose laws will govern the agreement. This is normally the franchisor's home state and can present a potentially difficult situation for you if you ever got into a legal hassle. For instance, if the franchisor selects Oregon and you're in Maine, resolving legal problems long distance could be quite expensive.
   b. *Notice.* This usually says that any required notices, like default, must be in writing and sent by certified or registered letter.
   c. *Waiver.* This says that if you or the franchisor violates one or several obligations, you can't assume the entire agreement is void or invalid.
   d. *Parties.* This section identifies you and the franchisor as the *only* parties to the agreement, not your friend, your spouse, or your lawyer.
   e. *Assignment.* This states that you can't assign, give, or sell the agreement to anyone else. However, the franchisor can, unless otherwise stated.

16. *More Reticals.* Some final "whereas's" and "now therefore's."

17. *Signatures, Dates, Witnesses.* Once you both sign the agreement, date it, and have it witnessed or notarized, it's in effect.

It may appear we've been a bit one-sided in our discussion, painting the franchisor as some kind of business Simon Legree. Most franchisors aren't evil taskmasters, but because it's *their* contract, they write it to protect themselves and not necessarily you. Again, read the agreement carefully, or take it to your attorney, heeding our previous warnings. As we mentioned, a franchisor's favorite defense is, "The government (meaning the FTC) won't let us change it," which simply isn't true: all the FTC requires is that the agreement must not be in conflict with the disclosure material. However, if you and/or your lawyer believe changes need to be made for you to be comfortable working with that franchisor, don't sign the contract until these differences are resolved. Above all, don't sign based on the franchisor's assurances that the changes you seek are just around the corner. We all know what happens to marriages when one or both partners enter the relationship with the idea the other will change, and usually change in a very specific way. Although such associations aren't necessarily doomed, their chances of being mutually successful are greatly limited from day one.

If you don't understand anything in the contract, ask to have it explained. If something bothers you, ask to have it changed or reworded so it doesn't. If the franchisor refuses for whatever reason, stop right there and carefully examine your *only* three options:

• Accept the contract as it exists and your negative feelings about it.

• Accept it, but change the way you feel about it.
• Look for another franchisor.

Although the first option might seem like the easiest, it's also the route taken by many of those who have been unsuccessful and/or unhappy franchisees. When you sign that contract, that's your way of saying you totally agree with every word that's in it. If you choose not to read it, to read things in it that aren't there or ignore things that are, you'll have a difficult (and expensive) time getting a court of law to support your views. It isn't the law or the FTC that guarantees what's in that contract is "right" and "legal"; it's your signature that makes it so.

Although you may initially find the idea of your signature carrying so much weight a bit frightening, it also gives you a lot of control over the situation. To be sure, once you sign you're legally bound to everything in that agreement. On the other hand, the franchisor has absolutely no power over you without your signature. Therefore, it's definitely to your advantage to take at least those ten days and go over all the disclosure material and the contract carefully. You want to feel absolutely sure that the responsibilities you retain for yourself and those you cede to the franchisor create what you consider the ideal business environment for you.

Now that we understand the implications of the FTC disclosure rules and how to evaluate a contract, let's look at some ways to analyze the franchisor's financial data.

CHAPTER 9

Using the Franchisor's Financial Data

INTRODUCTION

Many franchisors face a bit of a dilemma when it comes to providing financial data regarding what you can expect in terms of sales, salary, and profit. As we mentioned, the good ones often give estimates in terms of ranges—"You can expect sales from $150,000 to $300,000." If franchisors release information that shows excessively optimistic sales and earnings (salary plus profit), they might not only wind up with disgruntled franchisees whose performance falls short of the estimates, they may also run afoul of state or federal laws. However, being too conservative with the numbers won't attract the necessary franchisees to keep the franchisor in business. Recognizing the pitfalls of being either too optimistic or pessimistic in their projections, most franchisors find using ranges rather than specific values protects both them and the potential franchise buyer.

Looking at the franchisor's data, your first concern is most likely how much money you need to get into the franchise. As mentioned, your total initial investment may consist of some or all of the following:

1. The franchise fee.
2. Equipment, furniture, supplies, fixtures, lease-hold improvements, signs, vehicles—assets you need to operate the business but which, in and of themselves, produce little or no income.
3. Inventory for resale (not applicable to service businesses).
4. Working capital for three purposes:
   a. Initial start-up costs which include formative legal and accounting fees, insurance, utility and tax deposits, licenses, pre-opening advertising.
   b. Funds to pay the expenses of the business—employee wages, your salary, utilities, rent, maintenance, supplies—until the business passes its breakeven point, the point when income from sales just pays all those expenses.
   c. Costs associated with your training—lodging and meals primarily.
5. Purchase of any land and buildings (real estate), although this is so rare in smaller franchises as to be virtually non-existent. Much more often than not, franchisees rent any real estate necessary for their businesses.

From a business standpoint, there's no reason to invest in anything unless you can earn a profit from it. Your second concern, then, is the return on your investment. To analyze a return properly, we need a minimum of three estimated values from the franchisor:

1. Net sales. This represents the total amount of money you can expect to take in over one year less any adjustments for returned goods and allowances.
2. Your salary.
3. Profit. This means many things to many people; there's gross profit, profit before owner's salary, profit before tax, and so on. For our discussion, when we use the word profit, it means what's left after *everything* else has been paid—all the business expenses, your salary, federal income taxes, state taxes. So, in the words of the accountant, we are speaking of *net profit after tax*. When we use the word "earnings," it means the sum of your salary plus profit after tax. Remember, the profit is yours; you may take it out in additional salary, put it back into the business (improvements, more advertising), or give it to your favorite charity. Make sure that you know how the franchisors are defining any values they give you. Obviously if their sales value doesn't reflect any returns or allowances or if they give you gross profit figures and you view them as net profit after tax, any analysis you do could be quite misleading.

Let's begin our analysis by reviewing some of the commonly used accounting terms and what they mean. Below is an income statement which some call a "P and L," or profit and loss statement:

Net Sales	$300,000
Cost of Goods Sold	150,000
Gross Profit	$150,000
Less: Expenses	100,000
Owner's Salary	30,000
Profit Before Tax	$ 20,000
Federal and State Taxes	5,000
Net Profit After Tax	$ 15,000

We've already mentioned net sales and net profit after taxes; now let's look at the other items on this income statement:

1. Cost of Goods Sold. This item only appears if you're selling a product; it represents what you paid for what you sold. Obviously, if you're operating a service business such as tax prepara-

tion, you're selling your time and that has no *cost* associated with it.
2. Gross Profit. Also called gross margin or operating profit, it's merely the result of subtracting the cost of what you sold from what you sold it for.
3. Expenses. A list of expenses can become quite lengthy—insurance, uniforms, cleaning and maintenance, snow removal, repairs, local taxes, wages, benefits, advertising, insurance, professional fees, training, office supplies, vehicle expenses, lease payments, interest on loans, telephone, utilities, depreciation of assets. They represent continuing costs of running the business. Many, like your rent and utilities, have to be paid whether you have sales or not.
4. Owner's Salary. Technically, this is an expense of the business, but we've separated it so we can examine it in more detail.
5. Profit Before Tax. This is what's left after we subtract expenses and owner's salary from gross profit.
6. Federal and State Taxes. These are taxes levied directly against profit of the business, and do not include sales taxes, property taxes, and the like.

Looking at our income statement another way we might examine the business as follows:

$300,000	What the business took in.
$255,000	What it cost to run the business—cost of goods sold, expenses, taxes.
$ 45,000	Earnings available to the owner—salary plus profit.

Our numbers look pretty good, don't they? The owner "earned" $45,000, or 15 percent, on sales of $300,000 (15 percent of what the owner took in in sales directly came to him or her as earnings). But suppose the franchisee paid $1 million for this franchise. Is it a good investment? One way we can evaluate this is to see how long it would take for our franchisee to "make back" the investment if everything stayed the same from one year to the next. We can determine this by dividing the annual earnings into the franchise fee:

$$\frac{\$1,000,000}{\$ \quad 45,000} = 22^+ \text{ years}$$

It will take our franchisee over 22 years to make back the original investment; not a very good return considering he or she could place that

$1,000,000 in a 6 percent savings account and earn $60,000 a year without lifting a finger.

EXAMINING FINANCIAL DATA

Before we give you a simple way to analyze financial data, we need to make a few introductory remarks. First of all, it's important to recognize that most folks don't become self-employed for purely financial reasons. However, the financial information for any potential franchise does provide a way to compare one franchise opportunity to another on a uniform basis. The method of comparison we propose is a short-cut and as such doesn't strictly follow accepted accounting principles. Because of this, it should only be used to compare franchised businesses, and with the idea that the results are relative rather than absolute. Our goal is simply to provide a way you can compare one franchise opportunity with another, *not* to determine whether a single franchise is financially sound. Finally, you'll be using some of the information developed here to complete a full analysis of each franchise you're considering seriously in the next chapter.

We mentioned earlier that in most cases you personally don't need to have the total initial investment required to begin a franchise. To be sure, you need some of the investment in cash, and that varies from one franchisor to another. Very small franchises with low entry fees usually want the entire fee, in cash, all at one time. However, regardless of the magnitude of the franchise fee, if you don't have it all in cash, you're going to have to come up with the balance somehow. The most common outside sources are: franchisor financing, commercial bank loan, finance company, rich aunt, investors. Therefore, the first numbers you need to know are your total initial investment, how much of it you have in cash and how much you need to get from other sources.

Two other numbers we need to examine are the average franchise's sales and earnings. Most likely you'll be given a range; if so, just take the midpoint of the range for your analysis. For example, if the franchisor tells you you can expect sales between $150,000 and $300,000 use $225,000 as your value for the computations to come. However, bear in mind that such ranges can be misleading. If the franchisor in our example says sales range from $150,000 to $300,000, you have no way of knowing whether 19 of those 20 franchises made $150,000 while only one made $300,000. In such a situation your $225,000 average sales wouldn't be representative of what you can reasonably expect. It would be a more accurate figure if the franchisor gave you an average value for *all* franchises rather than a range reflecting only the two extremes.

Now let's take our values for a hypothetical franchise and see what we can do with them:

FRANCHISE:	Just Sew Fabrics
CASH REQUIRED:	$ 25,000
TOTAL INVESTMENT:	$ 60,000
SALES:	$400,000
EARNINGS:	$ 50,000

First, it's important we look at the numbers as they stand. For example, if you're considering Just Sew Fabrics, you need to have the 25 grand in cash. Furthermore, this better not be every cent you have because the business may not be able to pay you a salary for a while but you'll still have your own continuing personal expenses. (That's why we had you estimate your monthly living expenses a while back.) Secondly, you need to know where the other $35,000, the balance of your investment, is coming from. Lastly, you must be satisfied with the earnings (which for our purposes consist of your salary plus profit) recognizing you can't take all the profit for yourself. Some of it must be put back in the business if you want to succeed.

Now let's use our values to determine five different relationships or ratios we can use to compare one franchisor's data to another's. (Mathematically, a ratio is simply one number divided by another.)

The first relationship we're going to look at is that between cash and total investment. It tells you what percent of the total investment you personally need to have in cash.

$$\frac{\text{Cash}}{\text{Total Investment}} \times 100 = \frac{\$25,000}{\$60,000} \times 100 = 41.7 \text{ percent}$$

Next, let's examine the relationship between sales and total investment. Borrowing an accounting term, we'll call this investment "turnover." It tells us how many times our total investment "turns over" or can be divided into the annual sales. In general, the higher the ratio the better: it's better to have a low total investment in a high sales business than a large investment in one having minimal sales.

$$\frac{\text{Sales}}{\text{Total Investment}} = \frac{\$400,000}{\$60,000} = 6.7 \text{ times}$$

The third ratio, which is expressed in percent like our first one, relates earnings to sales. This tells us the return on sales or how much of the total sales come back to the franchisee as earnings. Please note this isn't the same as the classic "profit margin" because our value for earnings also includes your salary.

$$\frac{\text{Earnings}}{\text{Sales}} \times 100 = \frac{\$50,000}{\$400,000} \times 100 = 12.5 \text{ percent}$$

The earnings-to-total-investment ratio is our fourth calculation. It's also a turnover measurement and compares your total investment to your estimated annual earnings.

$$\frac{\text{Earnings}}{\text{Total Investment}} = \frac{\$50,000}{\$60,000} = 0.8 \text{ times}$$

Here again, the higher the number the better.

Finally, we're going to flip the fourth ratio upside down. This gives us the "payback"; the amount of time in years it takes those earnings to pay back your total investment. This figure won't be your *actual* payback because the earnings you get from the franchisor are from *going businesses,* those that are (hopefully) established and profitable. Your first year's earnings will undoubtedly be below this average. However, because we're using our ratios to compare one franchise to another rather than determine absolute values for one, this relationship serves our purposes quite well. We're not interested in the number of years it takes franchise A's earnings to pay back our total investment; we are interested in whether franchise A's payback is longer or shorter than Franchise B's or C's.

Our payback is:

$$\frac{\text{Total Investment}}{\text{Earnings}} = \frac{\$60,000}{\$50,000} = 1.2 \text{ years}$$

and that's about 14 months. This tells you you can expect a *minimum* of 1 year and 2 months to go by before you can recover your investment.

After all this number-crunching, we've generated a set of ratios that really don't mean much, because we have nothing to compare them to. However, if we're comparing the ratios of one franchise to another, they can tell us a great deal. In the table below we compare Just Sew with two other actual franchisors.

		Just Sew Fabrics	Franchisor #1	Franchisor #2
Cash Required	($)	25,000	15,000	6,800
Total Investment	($)	60,000	65,000	14,800
Sales	($)	400,000	215,000	85,000
Earnings	($)	50,000	54,700	38,800
Cash/Total Investment	(%)	41.7	23.1	45.9
Sales/Total Investment	(times)	6.7	3.3	5.7
Earnings/Sales	(%)	12.5	25.4	45.6
Earnings/Total Investment	(times)	0.8	0.8	2.6
Payback	(Years)	1.2	1.2	0.4

Let's see what we can learn by comparing our franchise data. Looking at Franchisor #1 and Just Sew, we see they have some similarities: the total investment is almost the same and earnings/total investment and payback are the same. But, Franchisor #1 may offer some advantages over Just Sew. For one thing, the cash required is $10,000 less, an important consideration for someone who wants or needs to conserve their initial cash. Of course, this means you'd have to consider financing $50,000 ($65,000 less $15,000) rather than only $35,000 with Just Sew. To give you an idea of what this might mean to your cash flow after you're in business, let's assume you borrow the balance in each case from a commercial bank; the interest rate is 14 percent and the term of the loan is 10 years. Here's what your monthly payment would be:

Just Sew:($35,000)	$543.43
Franchisor #1:($50,000)	$776.33
Difference:	$232.90 (or $2,794.80 per year)

So even though your initial investment in Franchisor #1 is $10,000 less, you must be sure it can generate enough earnings to handle those $232.90 higher monthly payments.

The major difference among our three franchisors occurs in their earnings/sales ratios. Franchisor #1's business earns twice as much as Just Sew percentagewise, and actually provides more earnings (in dollars) on less sales.

Franchisor #2 is a much smaller business, but look how "efficient" it is compared to the first two. Earnings/sales are extremely high in comparison and the theoretical payback occurs in one-third the time.

There is one more comparison we're going to make for Just Sew that you should make for any potential franchise candidates. We're going to look at comparable ratios for a group of franchises. It would be nice if we had ratios either for all franchises in the country or those for all fabric stores like Just Sew, but no data like this exists or, if it does, we haven't been able to find it. We analyzed nine national franchises for our compa-

rative ratios and used this information noting *very carefully* that a sample of nine out of 2,000 possible franchises isn't statistically sound. On the other hand, it does give us an idea how Just Sew *generally* stacks up to other franchises. Obviously, the more similar the franchises are in your comparison group, the more meaningful any differences will be. For example, if you're comparing franchises that are all in the same area, have about the same total investment and produce approximately the same earnings, these ratios can help you identify differences that may save or cost you money in the long run.

Here's how Just Sew compared to our averages:

	Just Sew Fabrics	Average of 9 Franchises
Cash/Total Investment (%)	41.7	53.1
Sales/Total Investment (times)	6.7	10.0
Earnings/Sales (%)	12.5	19.8
Earnings/Total Investment (times)	0.8	1.5
Payback (years)	1.2	0.7

We can see that Just Sew falls a bit short of the average franchise in our sample.

Both investment "turnovers" are lower (sales/total investment and earnings/total investment), earnings/sales are less, and its payback longer. Again, as long as you bear in mind that you're using this process to *compare* franchises you're interested in rather than statistically analyze a specific franchise for absolute values, this is a simple way to sort through financial data. On the next page we've provided a form to enter data on three franchises. We've put in our "standards" or averages for comparison as well.

Having spent an entire chapter on the analysis and comparison of financial data, you may be thinking these considerations are the only ones governing the selection of a franchise. However, that's not the case. In the next chapter we'll examine the other factors that should be considered before you make your final choice.

Item		Franchisor	Franchisor	Franchisor	Average of 9 Franchises
Cash Required	($)	————	————	————	
Total Investment	($)	————	————	————	————
Sales	($)	————	————	————	————
Earnings	($)	————	————	————	————
		————	————	————	————
Cash/Total Investment	(%)	————	————	————	53.1
Sales/Total Investment	(times)	————	————	————	10.0
Earnings/Sales	(%)	————	————	————	19.8
Earnings/Total Investment	(times)	————	————	————	1.5
Payback	(years)	————	————	————	0.7

CHAPTER 10

Reflection and Analysis

REFLECTION

Let's take a few minutes to look at where we've been and what we've learned. We began the process of finding a franchise by reading and responding to ads, writing to franchisors listed in the government's "Franchise Opportunities Handbook" and/or the IFA's membership list, and visiting franchise locations in your area. If you're like most potential franchisees you probably acquired information from five, ten, or even more franchisors and then narrowed your list to a manageable number. Once you had sufficient information to peak your interest, you began your travels—first to the franchisor's headquarters, then to more franchisee stores. Finally, you did some financial analysis to help narrow your choices even more, hopefully to more than one but less than six. Let's assume that you now have three good candidates. By "good" we mean:

- The basic idea of the business appeals to you.
- You have the experience to run the business or believe the franchisor will train you.
- The franchisor has a proven track record.
- You like the franchisor's people.
- You can afford the franchise.
- The franchise can support you.
- Running that business appears enjoyable.
- The financial analysis is sound.

Reflect on those eight qualities: be sure you're not misleading yourself. Now imagine yourself as the owner of each of the 3 businesses. Follow your activities in each business during a typical day as best as you can in your mind. Does one *feel* better than the others? Can you rank the three into your first, second, and third choice? If you can't do it right off the bat, try this:

For each choice, list the advantages and disadvantages *as you see them.* The fact that your brother-in-law considers the pest control franchise less classy than the gourmet deli isn't a disadvantage unless you share this opinion or his opinion is so important to you it could affect your success in the pest control business. Put down as many qualities as you can. When you complete your lists, go back and assign a value to each advantage and disadvantage—1, 2, and 3 for "not important," "mildly important," and "important," for example. Then add the values for all the advantages and all the disadvantages and see which total is greater. For example, when Gary Alper rated his positive and negative feelings about the pest control franchise, the positives scored 27 and the negatives 14.

A simpler way to examine your choices would be to take each franchise and give your strongest single reason for considering it and your strongest single reason for eliminating it. Then see if one outweighs the other. When Gary uses this method, his strongest positive reason is: "I feel I can really do well in this business." His strongest reason for not buying the franchise is: "A lot of folks are squeamish about bugs." When he views the franchise this way, Gary decides that his positive feelings about his ability to do the job plus his awareness of others' negative feelings about it actually strengthen his belief in this as the best franchise for him. The fact that he believes he can do a good job at something many others find repulsive tells him others are more likely to seek out his services than do the job themselves.

What you want to do here is express your personal feelings about your choices. Too many times business decisions and choices are made using cold, impersonal mathematics with little thought given to how we feel about those choices. If your heart's not in the business, it not only won't be much fun; you'll greatly increase your chances of failure.

From time to time we've heard people say they're really not sure whether they want a particular business or not. Well, there's a way to test the strength of that indecision—if someone could *give* you the business, would you take it? If your answer is either "no" or "not sure," then back away. If you're not sure you would want it if it were free, chances are you definitely wouldn't be happy with it if you had to pay for it.

ANALYSIS

The following pages contain a series of questions that enable you to review each franchise opportunity. You've answered some of the questions before; others are new. If you don't have the proper data to answer some of the questions, we suggest you contact the franchisor. We want you to experience as few surprises as possible and believe the information asked for is essential to properly evaluate any franchise. If the franchisor can't or won't provide the information, we suggest you drop them from your list.

The form has two parts. The first consists of questions to be answered "yes," "no," or "not sure." For any "not sure" responses, be sure you collect the necessary information to eventually answer them "yes" or "no." A "not sure" answer tells you nothing except that you need more information. The second part of the form asks for names, numbers, and written information.

FRANCHISE ANALYSIS FORM

Name of Franchisor:
Address:
City, State, Zip:

PART I

A. THE FRANCHISOR	Yes	No	Not Sure
1. Was I treated fairly and openly by the franchisor?	___	___	___
2. Do I believe the franchisor has met the spirit and intent of the FTC Rule?	___	___	___
3. Was I allowed to take my own time and not hustled?	___	___	___
4. Were people professional and qualified?	___	___	___
5. Do I think the franchisor is honest?	___	___	___
6. Were all my questions answered to my satisfaction?	___	___	___
7. Does the franchisor have a good reputation?	___	___	___
8. Is the franchisor financially sound?	___	___	___

	Yes	No	Not Sure

9. Are all the materials I've received clear and easy to understand? _____ _____ _____

10. Is the franchisor and its key people free from lawsuits? _____ _____ _____

11. Was I given
    a. FTC disclosure material? _____ _____ _____
    b. A copy of the agreement? _____ _____ _____
    c. Financial projections? _____ _____ _____
    d. References? _____ _____ _____

12. Is the franchisor a member of the IFA? _____ _____ _____

13. Is the franchisor listed in "Franchise Opportunities Handbook?" _____ _____ _____

14. Does the franchisor have a newsletter? _____ _____ _____

15. Does the franchisor have a toll-free number? _____ _____ _____

B. MARKETING/BUSINESS

1. Has the product or service proven to be a success? _____ _____ _____

2. Does the product or service seem to have staying power? _____ _____ _____

3. Is the industry (fast food, business services) growing? _____ _____ _____

4. Is the franchisor growing? _____ _____ _____

5. Is the franchisor national in its operations? _____ _____ _____

6. Do I think this franchise will go in my area? _____ _____ _____

7. Does this franchise fulfill my personal goals? _____ _____ _____

8. Does the franchisor have a national advertising program? _____ _____ _____

9. Does the franchisor help me with local advertising—either financially or by providing ad copy? _____ _____ _____

10. Does the franchisor have a customer service department to answer my questions? _____ _____ _____

11. If applicable, does the franchisor provide sales leads? _____ _____ _____

12. Did the franchisor give me an idea who or what my market is, who buys their products? _____ _____ _____

13. Do I know my competition well? _____ _____ _____

14. Does the franchisor have plans for new products and services? _____ _____ _____

15. Do I have an exclusive territory? _____ _____ _____

16. Is the product or service protected by patents, trademarks, copyrights? _____ _____ _____

C. OPERATIONS

1. Am I expected to work full-time at the business? _____ _____ _____

	Yes	No	Not Sure

2. May I operate the business from my home? _____ _____ _____

3. If the answer to (2) above is "no," may I lease the facility I need? _____ _____ _____

4. If the answer to (3) above is "no," does the franchisor help in the design, construction, furnishing or financing of the building? _____ _____ _____

5. Does the franchisor provide operations manuals? _____ _____ _____

6. May I buy equipment, supplies, and inventory from sources other than the franchisor? _____ _____ _____

7. Can I make a "good living" from this franchise? _____ _____ _____

8. Am I free to hire who I want? _____ _____ _____

9. Do the financial ratios (see previous chapter) appear sound? _____ _____ _____

D. CONTRACT

Are the following items covered in the franchisor's contract?

1. The franchise fee. _____ _____ _____
2. Royalties and commissions. _____ _____ _____
3. Requirement to purchase from franchisor. _____ _____ _____
4. Advertising payments. _____ _____ _____
5. My duties and responsibilities. _____ _____ _____
6. Franchisor's duties and responsibilities. _____ _____ _____
7. Territory. _____ _____ _____
8. Training. _____ _____ _____
9. Causes for termination. _____ _____ _____
10. Ability to renew. _____ _____ _____
11. Financing. _____ _____ _____
12. Escape clauses. _____ _____ _____

E. TRAINING

1. Is the cost of initial training included in the franchise fee? _____ _____ _____
2. Is this initial training sufficient for me to be able to run this business? _____ _____ _____
3. Does the franchisor offer continuing education beyond the initial training? _____ _____ _____

PART II

1. If the franchisor is a division or subsidiary of a larger company, what is the name and address of that company?

_____

2. Is the parent company, or the franchisor itself if there is no parent,
    a. A privately held company?   _____
    b. A publicly traded company?   _____
    c. If it's public, where is its stock traded?   _____
            New York Stock Exchange   _____
            American Stock Exchange   _____
            Other Stock Exchange   _____
            Over-the-Counter   _____

3. Concerning the franchise company,
    a. What year was it founded?   _____
    b. In what year was the first franchise
        opened?   _____
    c. What is the *total* number of franchise
        locations that have been opened?   _____
    d. How many company-owned locations are
        there?   _____
    e. How many *franchises* have failed?   _____
    f. Compute the franchisor's failure rate:

$$\frac{\text{No. of failures (2e.)}}{\text{No. of total locations (2c)}} \times 100 = \qquad \underline{\hspace{3cm}}\%$$

        NOTE: If this figure is 20 percent or above, we suggest you be extremely
              cautious about your consideration of this franchise.
    g. How many new franchises does the fran-
        chisor expect to sell in the next 12
        months?   _____
    h. Compute the growth rate for the next year:

$$\frac{\text{No. of planned franchises (2g)}}{\text{No. of total locations (2c)}} \times 100 = \qquad \underline{\hspace{3cm}}\%$$

        NOTE: If this figure is 100 percent or greater, be cautious. Too-rapid
              growth has buried many franchisors.

4. Give a brief description of the business as you understand it now.

5. What is the biggest advantage of this business?

6. What are its greatest drawbacks?

7. Below, list any positive or negative facts about this franchisor you've discovered in your research.

   a. Discussion with Franchisee #1.   Name: _____

   b. Discussion with Franchisee #2.   Name: _____

   c. Discussion with Franchisee #3.   Name: _____

   d. National Better Business Bureau Reports.

   e. FTC Publications.

   f. Local Better Business Bureau or Chamber of Commerce.

   g. Research in newspapers and magazines.

h. Other.

8. If you know the reasons for any failures, list them.

9. Consider the community where you're thinking of locating: list your competition (which can be both franchised and non-franchised businesses) and any appropriate comments—estimated sales, strong and weak points, years in operation.
   NOTE: The Yellow Pages are your best place to start.

Name of Competitor and Address	Comments
a.	
b.	
c.	
d.	
e.	

| Name of Competitor and Address | Comments |

f.

g.

10. What is the total franchise fee?
    $_____

11. How much of the initial fee must I pay before
    I begin?
    $_____

12. How much are my startup costs (equipment,
    inventory, supplies)?
    $_____

13. What do I need for working capital (money to
    run the business until it's profitable)?
    $_____

14. If applicable, how much will it cost to buy
    land and build a building?
    $_____

15. If there are any other funds required (special
    deposits, advance royalties, fees), how much
    are they?
    $_____

16. What is my total investment? (10. + 12. + 13.
    + 14. + 15.)
    $_____

17. If the franchisor provides financing, how
    much of the total (16., above) is covered?
    $_____

18. What interest rate does the franchisor
    charge?
    _____%

19. If the franchisor provides no financing, where can I go for it? (List banks,
    friends, relatives, investors.)
    a.

b.

c.

d.

20. How much, if any, of the initial fee will be
    refunded and under what circumstances?
    (For example, 100% refunded prior to train-
    ing, 80 percent within five days after complet-
    ing training.)
        $_____

21. Refer to your calculations in the previous chapter for the four items below:
    a. Cash required
        $_____
    b. Total investment
        $_____
    c. Sales
        $_____
    d. Earnings
        $_____

22. Next, record the five ratios:
    a. Cash/Total Investment
        _____%
    b. Sales/Total Investment
        _____times
    c. Earnings/Sales
        _____%
    d. Earnings/Total Investment
        _____times
    e. Payback
        _____years

23. What royalties do I pay and how are they computed? (8 percent of net sales,
    for example.)

24. If there are any other fees, costs, assessments, or charges (1% of sales for
    national advertising, $1,000 annual auditing fee), list them below:

25. According to the franchisor, how long will it be before the business "breaks even," and is self-sufficient? (If this figure is given in months or a combination of years and months, convert it to years expressed in decimals. For example, 18 months becomes 1.5 years.)

_____years
(expressed in decimals)

NOTE: Compare this to the theoretical payback (22c). It should be longer because the payback was calculated based on the earnings of an *established* business. The time to achieve the breakeven point is based on your starting from scratch.

26. How many people will I need to hire?

	Part-time	Full-time
a. To start with:		
b. After 1 year:		
c. After 2 years:		

27. Are there special skills or education my employees need to have?

Job Title	Skills/Education Needed
a.	a.
b.	b.
c.	c.
d.	d.

28. Who is my primary franchisor contact?

Name _____

Title _____

Address _____

City, State, Zip _____

Phone _____

29. List any other franchisor contacts available to help:

    a.

    b.

    c.

    d.

30. Rate this business from 1 (a total dog, wouldn't take it if someone paid me) to 10 (absolutely perfect in every way) based on how you personally feel about it.

                              Rating: _____

EXAMINING YOUR ANALYSIS

The Franchise Analysis Form is included in this book for two reasons: to provide a format for condensing important data, and to give you a method of comparing one franchise to another. Looking at 58 yes-no answers (Part I) and 30 other pieces of information (Part II) for every franchise seems a bit confusing, so let's condense some of it. Keep in mind that in summarizing the characteristics of the group, we're bound to lose sight of some of the individual details. However, tabulating the results this way does enable you to conveniently compare those franchises that interest you the most from personal and financial viewpoints.

Item		Franchisor	Franchisor	Franchisor
No. of "yes" answers in Part I (58 max.)		_____	_____	_____
Failure rate (3f)	(%)	_____	_____	_____
Growth rate (3h)	(%)	_____	_____	_____
Payback Time (22c)	(years)	_____	_____	_____
Time to Achieve Break-even Point (25)	(years)	_____	_____	_____
My rating (30) (1–10)		_____	_____	_____

Compare the payback time with the time the franchisor says it will take for your business to become self-sufficient. We already noted the latter will be larger than the former. If it isn't, beware: there's most likely some funny number juggling going on. On the other hand, be equally wary of a large gap between your calculated payback and the franchisor's estimated time to break even. Until the business is capable of supporting itself, any additional funds needed are going to have to come out of your pocket. Given a payback time of 1.5 years and a breakeven time of 1.0 years for franchise #1, and a payback time of 1.2 years and a breakeven time of 1.1 years for franchise #2, we're talking about a difference of 0.5 versus 0.1 year. Could you afford to support yourself and your business for an additional half-year if franchisor #1's time to break even was too optimistic? The difference between the theoretical payback time and the time to break even isn't time you will necessarily *have* to support yourself and your business beyond that estimated by the franchisor. However, it is time you *might* have to, and as such, the shorter the interval, the better.

Although we could have boiled even these categories down further such that each franchisor would wind up with a single number rating, we feel it's important you recognize where the major strengths and weaknesses of your choices lie. For some, the time required to become a fully operational business may carry more weight than the rate of growth. Others may find they're much more comfortable with a business having a low failure rate and will accept slower growth if necessary to get it. Still others will feel the more subjective qualities of the business and the franchisor reflected in Part I are much more important than any numerical analysis.

Regardless of your personal preferences, taking the time to analyze each franchise you're seriously considering using this system will keep that one preference from being your only one. We've seen businesses fail because they were based only on personal preferences, while others succumbed because their owners had a lot of data and no personal criteria. The successful business is invariably a harmonious combination of the two.

Now before you make that phone call or mail that signed contract and check, have your advisors—attorney, accountant, insurance agent, banker, consultant—at least in mind or, preferably, already on board. The next time you talk to them you'll no longer be speaking as a potential small business owner; the next time you'll *be* a small business owner.

In the next chapter we'll discuss financing and what little there is left to do before you're ready to open your doors.

CHAPTER 11

How You Buy a Franchise

Suppose you locate a franchise and a franchisor that meet all your requirements except one: you don't have enough of your own money to buy it. What should you do? That's a tricky question and the answer depends a lot on how you feel about money. For example, the thought of having to borrow money makes Cary Davidson feel vulnerable and uneasy. Even though his credit is excellent and most potential lenders would consider loaning him money merely a matter of paperwork, to him it adds a tremendous burden to the process of owning his own business. If his concern is sufficient to interfere with his enjoyment of the business, regardless how ideal in theory it may be, he'd be better off looking for something less expensive.

On the other hand, if you really believe a franchise is worth the price and the idea of borrowing doesn't frighten you, there are several different outside sources of cash you can consider.

MONEY

Basically there are two kinds of money you can use to buy your franchise. You can use your money and, if you don't have enough of that, you can use OPM—Other People's Money. However, *before* you sign that franchise agreement, make darn sure you know just *how* you're going to finance the franchise fee, equipment, inventory supplies, startup expenses, initial operating expenses (until the business makes a profit), and real estate if that's a consideration. It's not absolutely necessary that you have total approval on a commercial bank loan, for example, but you should know the source of potential OPM. If you're serious about Dolly's Dog Walking Service, which requires a total cash investment of $50,000, your proposed total financing picture might look like this:

My own investment	$18,000 (in savings account)
Loan from Dad	$ 7,000 (O.K. with Dad)
Commercial loan	$25,000 (see Julie at 1st National)

You should know just how much money you're going to need *and* that amount should include a healthy safety margin. If the franchisor says you can be profitable in six months, double that estimate; plan to run at a loss for one year. There are bound to be expenses neither you nor the franchisor ever thought of; the telephone deposit you thought was $150 suddenly becomes $350 because the phone company wants two months' estimated billing in advance. (They forgot to mention this when you talked to them last month.)

The easiest way to figure out everything in advance is to write a business plan or at least the financial part of one. We're not going to discuss business planning in this book because the theory and methods are well covered elsewhere. Our other book, *Buying Your Own Small Business,* (1985, The Stephen Greene Press) devotes an entire chapter to the subject and provides a detachable workbook ("Your Three-Year Business Plan For Buying a Small Business"). The U.S. Small Business Administration (SBA) also has business planning booklets available.

Let's assume you don't have all the money you need and therefore have to secure some OPM. The first possible source of OPM is most obviously the franchisor. By now you should know whether or not the franchisor will:

1. Provide all the financing you need.
2. Finance a portion of what you need.
3. Assist you in securing financing.
4. Leave the entire matter up to you.

Because we know franchisor financing is pretty rare, let's assume you have to find your own sources and types of financing.

SOME BACKGROUND

You do have a leg up when it comes to finding OPM for a franchise because many financing sources are positively predisposed, probably because of the success of the large, international franchisors. However, don't assume for a moment that you can breeze into a banker's office, ask for 50 grand, and be out of there with a check in half an hour. You're going to have to follow the same protocol as anyone else who's starting or buying a business. You must convince any financing source that *you* can operate the franchise successfully. Private investors, bankers, and finance company officials don't care much about the track record of other successful franchisees; they must be confident that you'll be a successful franchisee. And although it may seem unfair, even though the presence of other successful franchisees won't help you, a history of failed franchises could certainly work against you. Still, the decks are stacked in your favor, but knowing that shouldn't keep you from doing your fundraising in an honest, professional, and thorough fashion.

At this stage you may or may not have signed the franchisor's agreement. Although there are some plusses and minuses to being at one stage or the other before you go after OPM, it's best not to have signed. We suggest that because, if you fail to get financing, you won't be at risk in any way. Let's look at the worst case: You sign the agreement and mail it to the franchisor with a certified check for the franchise fee. Now you look for financing and come up empty-handed. You ask the franchisor for your money back and the franchisor says no. You could sue, but:

1. The franchisor is 2,000 miles away.
2. Your lawyer isn't licensed to practice in the franchisor's state so you either have to hire a stranger by phone or travel to that state, paying all your own expenses.
3. The new lawyer wants a sizeable retainer to begin the case.
4. The lawyer has only handled two cases involving franchising.
5. Every .01 hour (less than a minute) that attorney spends on the case costs you $1.00.
6. Chances are you'll lose the case (and *all* the money you've spent) because it's the franchisor's agreement and was drawn up by a roomful of lawyers immensely skilled in creating franchise agreement loopholes.

The other advantage to seeking OPM before you sign the franchise agreement is a more subtle one. Going to your bank, Dad, or Aunt Harriet after you've already committed to the franchise could make them think you want only their money, not their input. Although perhaps none of your potential lenders have sufficient background to adequately evaluate the franchise opportunity, the fact remains, no one likes to feel they're being pressured by circumstances—especially for money. Put yourself in their place. How would you feel if your brother signed on with Lavender Lace Lingerie Delights and wanted you to take a second mortgage on your service station to help him finance it?

FORM A CORPORATION

Although we haven't discussed what legal form your business should take, chances are your lawyer and the franchisor will suggest you form a corporation. There are several advantages to the corporation, as opposed to a sole proprietorship or a partnership. Some of these advantages are:

1. An unlimited life. Proprietorships and partnerships cease to exist when the principals die or become incapacitated.
2. Taxes. In a proprietorship or partnership you pay income taxes on the *combination* of salary and profit. With a corporation, you can break these two elements into personal tax (salary) and corporate tax (profit), thereby placing both categories into lower tax brackets. Usually this means a smaller overall tax bill.
3. Most states have simplified their corporate laws, making it possible to form one with you as the sole director, sole stockholder, sole officer.
4. Unlike proprietorships or partnerships, you may have limited personal liability for acts of the business. Suppose you own a restaurant and someone gets food poisoning, and sues. With a proprietorship or even a partnership, that person sues *you*. However, if you're a corporation, they sue the *corporation*, which in the eyes of the law, is a separate "person."
5. Corporations have more flexibility in raising money.

We're primarily interested in the last item: you can borrow in your corporation's name, although you'll have to personally guarantee any loans. A corporation can also raise *equity* funds by selling stock (ownership) in the corporation.

EQUITY FUNDS

You've undoubtedly heard the word equity before, probably in relation to the home you own. If the market value of the house and land is $100,000 and the balance on the mortgage is $30,000, you have an equity in your property of $70,000. In other words, if the house sells for $100,000, the bank gets 30 grand and you get 70.

Suppose you want a $10,000 car but need a loan to help you buy it. In order to get that loan, you need some money of your own. Let's say the bank or finance company wants 20 percent down, or $2,000. If you have the 2 grand, that's your *equity* investment. The bank then loans you the other

$8,000. If you don't have the "downer," you may have to go to Aunt Sadie for the difference.

Businesses, including franchises, are often financed the same way. But how much of your own money will you need? That depends on several factors—type of franchise, track record of that franchise, amount of collateral available to be pledged as security, competitive situation, bank policies, economic conditions—but the range is usually 25 to 40 percent of the total. Most bankers or other financial institutions won't go for a deal where the debt-to-equity ratio is greater than 2:1. This means you need to have at least one-third or 33⅓ percent of the total cash investment in the form of equity before they will consider lending you the rest.

Let's look at an example. Suppose the economy is a bit tight and your local commercial bank tells you they won't consider your franchise unless the debt-to-equity ratio is 1.5:1 or less. Let's also assume you need a total of $25,000. Therefore, if

$$\frac{\text{debt}}{\text{equity}} = 1.5$$

and

$$\text{debt} + \text{equity} = \$25,000$$

by substituting, we see

$$1.5 \text{ equity} + \text{equity} = \$25,000$$
$$2.5 \text{ equity} = \$25,000$$
$$\text{equity} = \frac{\$25,000}{2.5} = \$10,000$$

and then because

$$\text{debt} = \text{total needed} - \text{equity}$$
$$\text{debt} = \$25,000 - \$10,000$$
$$\text{debt} = \$15,000$$

To double-check

$$\frac{\text{debt}}{\text{equity}} = \frac{\$15,000}{\$10,000} = 1.5$$

Therefore, the bank is willing to loan you $15,000 (60 percent of $25,000) of what you need if you come up with $10,000 or 40 percent. If you have $6,000 yourself, you need to raise the other four thousand from equity investments. Although you can get advice from your banker in advance, you should have your equity before going to the bank for additional financing.

Talk with friends and relatives as equity investors before you approach strangers. Although not always the case, most people are more at ease stating their case to those they know well and are therefore able to do a better job. Furthermore, friends and relatives are more likely to be aware of those qualities which, while beneficial in your proposed business (your great sense of humor, your patience, or adaptability), can't be expressed adequately on financial forms.

Strangers willing to back you financially are usually men and women who are well off financially and looking for a *sound* investment. You can find out names of such potential investors from:

- Your banker
- Your accountant and attorney
- The local chamber of commerce
- The local industrial development group
- An SBA representative
- Your stockbroker
- Your insurance agent

You can also advertise in newspapers, but be sure to check with your lawyer for the correct wording. There are securities laws enacted to protect folks from scams; you won't run afoul of these if you follow your attorney's advice and explain to potential investors just what they're investing in. Your franchise agreement usually satisfies the legal requirements for "informing an investor."

We're going to discuss the corporate form of equity (buying stock) as opposed to the partnership form of equity (limited partners) because it's more common. When you take in equity, you usually sell shares of common stock. What happens when you sell common stock?

- You sell ownership.
- You provide your stockholder(s) with a stock certificate or other proof of ownership.
- You give your stockholder(s) voting privileges, usually one vote for each share of common stock.

How do you place a value on the stock of a franchise? You get the advice of the franchisor as well as your accountant and attorney. What you're selling is an investment opportunity. Although dear Aunt Sadie wants to help you because you're her favorite niece, she must be shown what happens to her investment if the business succeeds or fails.

Let's assume you have $6,000 and need $4,000 in outside equity. Let's say Aunt Sadie is your outside stockholder and you each purchase stock at $1 per share. You then own 6,000 shares and your aunt 4,000. Because you have 60 percent of the votes and she has 40 percent, you have what is known as the controlling interest; that is, you own more than 50 percent of the corporation. It is *generally* a good idea to maintain this control because if you don't, you can be voted out of your own corporation.

How can we make this $4,000 a good investment for Aunt Sadie? Some people think they'll pay dividends on the stock, but that's extremely rare in small business. In the first place, the business needs every bit of cash it can use. Secondly, dividends come under what's known as double taxation; they're taxable to the corporation *and* the recipient. What you'll probably do is buy out Aunt Sadie when:

1. The business grows and has several profitable years under your management;
2. The business can afford to do so either through the accumulation of a reserve fund or by borrowing.

Maybe in five years the value of Aunt Sadie's (and your) stock goes from $1 to $3 a share. If you and your aunt have the proper legal agreement, you pay her $12,000 for her 4,000 shares. She triples her money in five years. Not bad! When you buy her out, you then own 6,000 shares, or 100 percent, of the corporation. Aunt Sadie's stock returns to the corporation and becomes treasury stock, that which was once issued and is now repurchased. It sits in the *treasury* and can be re-issued without changing the bylaws.

If you can't buy out Aunt Sadie, she remains a stockholder until something happens. That "something" could be her death, in which case you might have to satisfy her heirs. Maybe they want cash and not some green certificate with naked people on it. Or that something could be the sale of the franchise. In any case, you need legal assistance. Your lawyer may suggest restricted stock; Aunt Sadie might be a sweet person who doesn't understand business, but you don't want her selling her stock to some sharpie who's only going to be a lot of trouble to you. If you sell her restricted stock, she signs an agreement not to sell her stock, or at least to give you first right of refusal, if she gets an offer to sell.

If you need to go beyond the Aunt Sadies of the world, you'll wind up talking with individuals who are fairly knowledgeable about business. Here are some guidelines for you:

1. If you're asked a question and don't know the answer, say so. Don't fumble through. Tell the person you'll get the information for them as soon as possible.
2. The really good investor certainly wants a return on his or her investment, but usually understands risk.
3. Investors will look at you more than at the business idea: successful *people* run successful businesses.
4. If one or several of these potential investors seems to be something other than honest and forthright, back off.

You may want to hold an open meeting at the local Holiday Inn to present your business opportunity to a number of people at one time. There's nothing wrong with this or with putting an ad in the paper to announce your meeting. If you do it this way, be sure you:

• Don't make any outrageous claims like saying this is the investment opportunity of a lifetime,
• Don't use any approach that looks like a Florida land sale,
• Have copies of the FTC material, franchise agreement, and your business plan available for all,
• Have your attorney, accountant, and banker at the meeting, and possibly someone from the franchise itself,
• Make the presentation. Your advisors can help clarify certain technical points, but it's *your* show,
• Are honest. If you discuss opportunity, also discuss risk, and
• Have charts or other visual aids to help make major points.

One other valuable consideration is the creation of an escrow account for stockholder investments. Your attorney will probably tell you it's not a good idea to start spending your stockholders' money before all the financing is in place. Because one reason you're using equity is to leverage a bank loan, open an escrow account (preferably at the bank you hope to do business with) for these funds so your stockholders' money can be returned to them in full if you fail to secure the loan.

BANKS AND BANK FINANCING

Few books on franchising spend much time on commercial lending and lending practices. Others try to teach you how to outwit or even bully a banker, painting the banker as uncaring, stingy, and stupid. We admit there are lousy bankers, just as there are lousy franchisors and franchisees, but if you approach a bank with the attitude you must beat the money out of them, you're going to have a rough time indeed. Commercial banks (usually the ones with "National" in their names) make most of their money from sound business loans. Of course they want that loan secured with collateral, but they don't want to go after that security in the case of default. They don't *want* your business, your house, or your car; that's a hassle for them and they're never certain they'll get their money back. They want the loan repaid *in accordance with its provisions*. That's only fair to them, and it's the best deal for you as well. If the loan has fixed payments over some period of time, you plan that as a fixed cost of running your business. No other cost you have stays that uniform.

We're going to examine what banks are looking for and what turns them off. Remember one thing: banks are run by people—they hope, they fear, they laugh, they cry. A banker probably worries about his checkbook balance or wants her kids to succeed in school. They have operating rules as you do, as the franchisor does.

One question we must consider is whether a bank looks more favorably on your purchasing a franchise or starting your own business. The answer is, "It depends." If they've never heard of the franchise, if you're personally unknown to them, if the local market already has too many businesses, franchised or non-franchised, you may face the same conditions as anyone just starting out.

WHAT DO BANKS LOOK FOR?

A bank is a very special kind of creditor, always looking for the "six C's" of credit:

1. *Character.* Who's borrowing this money? Businesses don't borrow and repay money, people do. If you seriously ran afoul of the law, if you defaulted on past obligations, or if your overall reputation is in question, you probably face an uphill battle. Bankers also assess you as a person. Do you seem to know what you're doing? Are you enthusiastic about your new franchise business? Do you demonstrate confidence?

2. *Cause.* What is the money being used for? What type of business? Every bank has its own list of no-no's. One kind of no-no pertains to how the money will be used. You can't just borrow money, stick it in the corporate checkbook, and pay yourself some extravagant salary. Banks understand that some money must stay in the form of cash, but most of it should go for real things—renovations, equipment, inventory. The other no-no involves the type of business. Although you may find some variation from one bank to another, bankers are nervous about:
   a. Anyone planning to open more than one franchised location at the same time. Although many individuals eventually own several franchises, these were usually opened over a period of time.
   b. Any business starting out with already established heavy competition.
   c. Fads.
   d. Businesses which, in their opinion, are high-risk or unethical.

3. *Capacity.* This refers to your ability or capacity to repay the loan. If you've completed a full business plan or even cash flow estimates based on information provided by the franchisor, you should be able to demonstrate how your loan repayment fits in with income and expenses. Most bankers feel the biggest borrowing shortcoming on the part of entrepreneurs is their failure to answer the question, "How will this loan be repaid?"

Because the loan repayment must be made from sales, most bankers will ask how you arrived at your projected sales total. If the franchisor's data is sound, you have a ready, logical, defendable answer. You may also have to face the fact that there are those bankers who simply refuse to accept your or the franchisor's figures.

4. *Collateral.* Unless you're related to J. Paul Getty, no bank will grant an unsecured loan. You must show how your loan will be secured (collateralized).

5. *Capital.* What is the net worth of the borrower? How much capital is the franchise owner putting into the business? What other equity capital is being supplied? By whom?

6. *Conditions.* As you know, the economy is always changing. During the early 1980s, business loans were difficult to secure and interest rates were hovering around 20 percent. When credit loosens up, banks become more competitive, capital is easier to come by, and it's cheaper.

In addition to the "six C's," additional business considerations that help sway a bank are:

- A demonstrated need for the franchise. Although the present market is reaching saturation, a computer retail store in the early 1980s certainly met this criterion.
- Established guidelines. Naturally, any well-established franchise (McDonald's, Pizza Hut) can point to a high degree of success because it isn't selling a clever way to make hamburgers or pizza, but rather a proven management method.
- A guarantee over and beyond collateral. This could be a co-signer to your loan who is reasonably well-off, or it could be a loan guarantor like the franchisor or the SBA.

What banks look for in you is:

- Someone who's truly committed to and enthusiastic about the business. Good bankers can easily spot folks on ego trips.
- A person who appears to be smart and logical. You don't have to be the resident genius but you must demonstrate you know what you're talking about.
- Experience. There are two kinds of experience: general business knowledge and a background in the type of franchise you're buying. Having neither

probably dooms your loan approval. One is fine. Both are great! Financial experience is especially prized.

Things that *absolutely* turn a bank (or a successful franchisor, for that matter) off include:

- A poor personal credit history. This doesn't mean simply missing a payment here and there. However, if you've had a car repossessed, a mortgage foreclosed, or if you've been through business or personal bankruptcy, it's going to be tough. On a lesser scale, judgments against you or liens on any of your assets can also cloud the issue.
- A criminal record. Of course, the nature of the crime and nature of the sentence, if any, do enter in. It's one thing if you were detained in the slammer for one night for some domestic issue but quite another if you embezzled bank funds.
- No cash. If you have no equity whatsoever, either personal or invested by others, forget it.

GETTING READY TO GO TO THE BANK

Your preparation for your meeting with a commercial loan officer is more important than the actual meeting itself. Bankers tell us they're appalled at the number of people who wander in off the street without an appointment, with little or no preparation, and ask for a business loan. This approach might work with a loan shark, but don't *ever* try it with a bank. You'll get a quick and possibly not-so-polite refusal. Respect the banker and show him or her normal business courtesies.

If you don't already have a relationship with a commercial bank, you need to target your choice. Your accountant can suggest one or two banks and you can also ask other business owners. Pick your first choice and one or two as backup. First obtain the name and title of the appropriate officer who handles commercial loans. In very small banks this may be the president, in medium-sized banks you'll probably be referred to one of the commercial loan officers, possibly even the head of the commercial loan department, and in larger banks it may be the manager of the branch bank nearest you. In some cases you may wind up with a junior officer, but it's important to deal with the designated person. If you jump the chain of command within the bank, you may jeopardize your case right from the beginning.

Regarding dealing with more than one bank: "Shopping the loan" should only be done under certain conditions, and then with care. Bankers say that if you have "the deal of the century" then you're probably well-advised to go to several banks, BUT make sure you inform each banker about the others. If you have some phenomenal situation, you can look for the most favorable terms and may even engage in a little negotiating (notice we said negotiating, not holding an auction) between banks. If your situation is average or marginal, shopping only hurts. A banker's attitude is, "Since this deal isn't the most attractive, why should I spend all the time processing the application only to have some other bank take it. The heck with it."

The next step is for *you* (not your accountant and especially not your attorney) to call the proper person at the bank. Introduce yourself, talk briefly about the business and the amount of money you need. Be certain the banker knows this is a franchise and neither the purchase of a going concern nor a business expansion. You may get turned down on the phone; if that happens, ask the person if he or she has any suggestions. Thank them for their time.

If you get an appointment, *ask* the officer if it's OK to bring along your accountant and/or the franchisor's representative. DO NOT bring your attorney, and *never* bring more than three people. Most bankers feel lawyers only muddy up the first meeting because they often attempt to overprotect their client. Banks have certain issues they won't budge on, and having a lawyer sit there arguing extraneous details only slows the process, frustrates the banker, and costs you money to boot. It may also kill the deal.

Tell the banker you have a business plan or financial data and ask what else you should bring. Bankers vary considerably on this. If this is the first meeting, it may be a get-acquainted session or what one bank president calls "mutual seduction." Chances are, though, the banker may also want:

- copies of your income tax returns for the past three years;
- your business lease agreement if you've signed one;

- insurance documents (life, casualty);
- some bank forms filled out in advance: e.g., a personal financial statement. See the next two pages for a widely used form. The bank is especially interested in credit references and your social security number;
- the personal financial statement of anyone acting as co-signer or loan guarantor;
- certificate of incorporation (if corporation), partnership agreement (if partnership);
- a list of investors (stockholders, limited partners) showing amounts of investment;
- all the franchisor's information;
- a list of collateral, including market values of homes, stocks, bonds.

How do you determine collateral for a business loan? Let's look at a potential franchisee who wants to buy a sporting goods franchise specializing in bicycling called "Full Cycle." First let's look at what our franchisee has to offer and what the market value of those assets are:

Item	Market Value
1. Single-family residence located at 23 Elm Street, first mortgage held by Consumer Savings Bank. Mortgage balance on 6/1/xx, $27,324.97 Property appraised by Robert Scranton, MAI, 6/10/xx	$42,500.00
2. Fifty common shares of IBM Corp. Value taken at close 6/8/xx, 102¼	5,112.50
3. Opening inventory—bicycles and parts. Value at cost on opening day	18,900.00
4. Equipment (at cost):	
a. Machines and tools	6,200.00
b. Furniture and fixtures	2,300.00
c. Cash register	1,895.00
Total	$76,907.50

Now let's look at the collateral for Full Cycle, Inc., and see how a bank might evaluate it for loan purposes. We say "might" because things vary with time and between banks.

1. *The house.* First, the bank determines the equity in the home by subtracting the mortgage from the market value:

$42,500.00
− 27,324.97
$15,175.03

By taking some part of the balance, usually between 70 and 90 percent, the actual value to the bank is determined. We'll use 80 percent and round off results to the nearest dollar.

80% × $15,175.03 .... $12,140.00

2. *The stock.* IBM is considered a "blue chip" security and therefore the bank accepts 75 percent of its total value for collateral. The value is lower on less stable securities and higher for U.S. government obligations (notes, bonds, bills).

75% × $5112.50   3,834.00

3. *Inventory.* 50 percent of the total is normal figure used.

50% × $18,900.00   9,450.00

4. *Equipment.*
a. Machines and tools: 60% × $6,200.00   3,720.00
b. Furniture & fixtures: 40% × $2,300.00   920.00
c. Cash register: 70% × $1,895.00   1,327.00

Total $31,391.00

Our cycling entrepreneur can probably secure a $30,000 loan with his collateral.

Other sources of collateral include:

- mortgages on business real estate;
- warehouse receipts (items placed in a public warehouse);
- trust receipts for floor planning (used for items such as appliances, boats, automobiles, power equipment);
- accounts receivable;
- life insurance if it has cash surrender value;
- savings accounts;
- the guarantee of another person (e.g., a wealthy individual who may also be a stockholder; your parents).

You can't collateralize things like irrevocable trusts or the fact that you're mentioned in Uncle Harold's will, however, because neither can be converted to cash on demand.

PERSONAL FINANCIAL STATEMENT

IMPORTANT: Read these directions before completing this Statement.

☐ If you are applying for individual credit in your own name and are relying on your own income or assets and not the income or assets of another person as the basis for repayment of the credit requested, complete only Sections 1 and 3.

☐ If you are applying for joint credit with another person, complete all Sections providing information in Section 2 about the joint applicant.

☐ If you are applying for individual credit, but are relying on income from alimony, child support, or separate maintenance or on the income or assets of another person as a basis for repayment of the credit requested, complete all Sections, providing information in Section 2 about the person whose alimony, support, or maintenance payments or income or assets you are relying.

☐ If this statement relates to your guaranty of the indebtedness of other person(s), firm(s) or corporation(s), complete Sections 1 and 3.

TO:

SECTION 1 - INDIVIDUAL INFORMATION (Type or Print)	SECTION 2 - OTHER PARTY INFORMATION (Type or Print)
Name	Name
Residence Address	Residence Address
City, State & Zip	City, State & Zip
Position or Occupation	Position or Occupation
Business Name	Business Name
Business Address	Business Address
City, State & Zip	City, State & Zip
Res. Phone Bus. Phone	Res. Phone Bus. Phone

SECTION 3 - STATEMENT OF FINANCIAL CONDITION AS OF _____ 19 ____

ASSETS (Do not include Assets of doubtful value)	In Dollars (Omit cents)		LIABILITIES	In Dollars (Omit cents)	
Cash on hand and in banks			Notes payable to banks - secured		
U.S. Gov't. & Marketable Securities - see Schedule A			Notes payable to banks - unsecured		
Non-Marketable Securities - See Schedule B			Due to brokers		
Securities held by broker in margin accounts			Amounts payable to others - secured		
Restricted or control stocks			Amounts payable to others - unsecured		
Partial interest in Real Estate Equities - see Schedule C			Accounts and bills due		
			Unpaid income tax		
Real Estate Owned - see Schedule D			Other unpaid taxes and interest		
Loans Receivable			Real estate mortgages payable - see Schedule D		
Automobiles and other personal property					
Cash value-life insurance-see Schedule E			Other debts - itemize:		
Other assets - itemize:					
			TOTAL LIABILITIES		
			NET WORTH		
TOTAL ASSETS			TOTAL LIAB. AND NET WORTH		

SOURCES OF INCOME FOR YEAR ENDED _____, 19____		PERSONAL INFORMATION
Salary, bonuses & commissions	$	Do you have a will?_____if so, name of executor.
Dividends		
Real estate income		Are you a partner or officer in any other venture? If so, describe.
Other income **(Alimony, child support, or separate maintenance**		
income need not be revealed if you do not wish to have it		Are you obligated to pay alimony, child support or separate maintenance payments? If so, describe.
considered as a basis for repaying this obligation)		
		Are any assets pledged other than as described on schedules? If so, describe.
TOTAL	$	
CONTINGENT LIABILITIES		
Do you have any contingent liabilities? If so, describe.		Income tax settled through (date)_____
		Are you a defendant in any suits or legal actions?
As indorser, co-maker or guarantor?	$	Personal bank accounts carried at:
On leases or contracts?	$	
Legal claims	$	
Other special debt	$	Have you ever been declared bankrupt? If so, describe.
Amount of contested income tax liens	$	

(COMPLETE SCHEDULES AND SIGN ON REVERSE SIDE)

SCHEDULE A - U.S. GOVERNMENTS & MARKETABLE SECURITIES

Number of Shares or Face Value (Bonds)	Description	In Name Of	Are These Pledged?	Market Value

SCHEDULE B - NON-MARKETABLE SECURITIES

Number of Shares	Description	In Name Of	Are These Pledged?	Source of Value	Value

SCHEDULE C - PARTIAL INTERESTS IN REAL ESTATE EQUITIES

Address & Type Of Property	Title In Name Of	% Of Ownership	Date Acquired	Cost	Market Value	Mortgage Maturity	Mortgage Amount

SCHEDULE D - REAL ESTATE OWNED

Address & Type Of Property	Title In Name Of	Date Acquired	Cost	Market Value	Mortgage Maturity	Mortgage Amount

SCHEDULE E - LIFE INSURANCE CARRIED, INCLUDING N.S.L.I. AND GROUP INSURANCE

Name Of Insurance Company	Owner Of Policy	Beneficiary	Face Amount	Policy Loans	Cash Surrender Value

SCHEDULE F - BANKS OR FINANCE COMPANIES WHERE CREDIT HAS BEEN OBTAINED

Name & Address Of Lender	Credit In The Name Of	Secured Or Unsecured?	Original Date	High Credit	Current Balance

(USE ADDITIONAL SCHEDULES IF NECESSARY)

The information contained in this statement is provided for the purpose of obtaining, or maintaining credit with you on behalf of the undersigned, or persons, firms or corporations in whose behalf the undersigned may either severally or jointly with others, execute a guaranty in your favor. Each undersigned understands that you are relying on the information provided herein (including the designation made as to ownership of property) in deciding to grant or continue credit. Each undersigned represents and warrants that the information provided is true and complete and that you may consider this statement as continuing to be true and correct until a written notice of a change is given to you by the undersigned. You are authorized to make all inquiries you deem necessary to verify the accuracy of the statements made herein, and to determine my/our creditworthiness. You are authorized to answer questions about your credit experience with me/us.

Signature (Individual) _____

S S No _____ Date of Birth_____

Signature (Other Party)_____

S S No _____ Date of Birth_____

Date Signed_____ 19_____

Once you have the necessary information to-gether, there are two things to do before the meeting. One is to be sure of your attitude. Be positive about the outcome of the meeting (even if you don't get the loan), your franchise, the business proposition, and most of all, yourself. Remember, you're presenting a situation that's mutually profitable to you and to the bank, monetarily and otherwise. You're not asking them to give you something for nothing.

The second thing is to be sure your presentation is clear, logical, and concise. Don't memorize a "pitch" but do think through what you want to say. You'll be asked probing questions such as:

Is the franchisor successful? Why?
• What makes you think this business will make it?
• What will you do if a new competitor opens up?
• Why have you chosen this location?
• Who are your employees? Suppliers? Customers?
• What business experience do you have?

THE MEETING ITSELF

It's the big day! You're going to meet a person whose dual dedication is (1) to help people in small business, and (2) to maintain the financial integrity of his or her business. A balance must exist for the bank to exist. If you've done your homework, the meeting will be a piece of cake. You'll be miles ahead of most others competing for the bank's money.

Be certain to dress for the occasion; a business suit is best.

Remember, *you* make the presentation. If your accountant or franchise representative is present, he or she can answer questions, but should not make any lengthy discourse.

After the presentation and any questions, one of three things will happen:

• You'll be turned down.
• You'll be asked to provide more information.
• You'll be told that the bank will consider the deal.

If you are turned down you have the right to ask two questions:

1. Why was I turned down?
2. What do I have to do to get the loan?

Listen carefully to both answers. By all means, don't walk out in a huff. Thank the banker honestly for his or her time and advice and either look for another bank or begin making the necessary changes.

If you're asked for more information (detailed résumé, loan application form, financial data), tell the bank when he or she can expect to have it. There is a sample business application form on the next two pages that gives you an idea what kinds of additional information they may require.

If you're told the bank needs time to consider the deal, ask when you can expect a final answer. The normal time is two weeks, but it could take longer. The bank will check your personal back-ground and analyze your proposal. They will check out the franchisor if they've never heard of it. If the analysis is satisfactory, your proposal is presented at the weekly meeting of the loan committee. The decision of that committee de-pends on:

• The history of the franchisor and its franchisees;
• The soundness of your proposal;
• Data the bank has generated studying your proposal;
• Conditions in the local economy;
• The number of loans outstanding, especially in franchises or your kind of business;
• The bank's cash position;
• Current government policies on loans.

If all is positive, you get your loan. A truly professional banker may suggest additional fi-nancing, either an increase in the loan or a line of credit, which is an already approved loan that you don't use unless you need to.

There are still some bankers who think it's necessary to talk someone down on a loan. This isn't the same as an honest banker who analyzes your cash flow projections and finds errors in either judgment or arithmetic and tells you your loan request is excessive. We're speaking of an arbitrary reduction for no sound reason. Don't go for this; it can only spell disaster. If your business plan is done carefully, it shows what you need. Taking less only causes the business to fail. You're not haggling over a used car.

APPLICATION
Small Business Term Loan

TO: THE FIRST NATIONAL BANK OF ANYTOWN. Date ....

The undersigned hereby submit(s) application for a loan in the net amount of

.... Dollars $ [   ]

For the purpose of ....

....

....

to be repaid in .... monthly payments on the □5th □10th □15th □20th □25th □30th day of the month.

BUSINESS RECORD
□ Corporation
□ Partnership

Name of Business .... □ Proprietorship
(Please Print)

Kind of Business .... Phone No. ....

Address ....
(Street)   (City or Town)   (Zone)   (State)
Year Business Established .... Annual Rent $ .... Lease Expires ....

Business Checking Account ....
(Name of Bank)

PRINCIPALS

Name.. Date of Birth ....

Residence ....

Residence Telephone No. .... No. of years at present residence ...... Number of Dependents ....

Previous Residence ....

Checking a/c (bank) .... Title of account .... Balance $ ....

Savings or Cooperative a/c (bank) .... a/c no .... Balance $ ....

Real Estate Owned .... Date Purchased .... Mtge. held by ....

| | Original | Present | Monthly | Rental |
Cost $ .... Valuation $ ..... Mortgage $ ..... Balance $ .... Payments $ ...... Income $ ....

Life Insurance: Face Amt. Carried $ .... Cash Value $ .... Subject to Loan of $ ....

Other Assets: Securities Mkt. Value $ .... Auto (Make & Year) ....

Open loans To Whom Owed	Original Amount	Unpaid Balance	Monthly Payment	Collateral
.... $	$	$		
.... $	$	$		

Name .... Date of Birth ....

Residence ....

Residence Telephone No. .... No. of years at present residence ..... Number of Dependents ....

Previous Residence ....

Checking a/c (bank) .... Title of account .... Balance $ ....

Savings or Cooperative a/c (bank) .... a/c no .... Balance $ ....

Real Estate Owned .... Date Purchased .... Mtge. held by ....

| | Original | Present | Monthly | Rental |
Cost $ .... Valuation $ ..... Mortgage $ ..... Balance $ .... Payments $ ...... Income $ ....

Life Insurance: Face Amt. Carried $ .... Cash Value $ .... Subject to Loan of $ ....

Other Assets: Securities Mkt. Value $ .... Auto (Make & Year) ....

Open loans To Whom Owed	Original Amount	Unpaid Balance	Monthly Payment	Collateral
.... $	$	$		
.... $	$	$		

Borrower, in consideration of Bank making the loan to Borrower, hereby warrants, represents and agrees as follows:

1. If Borrower is a corporation, Borrower is duly organized and existing under the laws of ....
and is duly qualified as a foreign corporation in the States of ....

2. Borrower will cause the following present indebtedness of Borrower to be subordinated to the loan by a Subordination Agreement satisfactory to Bank.

Name of Creditor of Borrower	*Amount*
....	....
....	....
....	....
....	....

3. The execution, delivery and performance hereof and any security instruments or guarantees called for or delivered hereunder are (if Borrower is a corporation) within its corporate powers, have been duly authorized, are not in contravention of the terms of Borrower's Articles of Incorporation or By-laws or any amendment thereof and (whether or not Borrower is a corporation) are not in contravention of law or of any indenture, agreement or undertaking to which Borrower is a party or by which Borrower is bound.

4. All financial statements, profit and loss statements, statements as to ownership and other statements heretofore or hereafter given to bank in connection with this agreement are or will be true and correct subject to any limitation stated therein and Borrower is the owner of all property in which Borrower has given or is giving a security interest to Bank, free from all encumbrances and Borrower will so own all property in which Borrower hereafter gives a security interest to Bank.

5. Borrower will maintain executive personnel and management satisfactory to Bank.

6. Borrower will maintain adequate fire (including so-called extended coverage), public liability and other insurance as Bank may require, in such form and written by such companies as may be satisfactory to Bank and will upon request of Bank deliver to it the policies concerned. All policies covering property given as security for the loan shall have a loss payable clause in favor of Bank.

GENERAL INFORMATION

Has the business, or any of the principals ever been involved in any judgments, attachments or other legal proceedings other than divorce, custody, alimony or separate support proceedings?

☐ Yes ☐ No If "yes" attach memorandum giving details.

Name of Accountant: .... Tel. No. ....

Address: ....

Name of Insurance Agent: .... Tel. No. ....

Address: ....

The foregoing statements and any supplementary information are warranted by the undersigned to be true and are furnished to induce you to make the loan applied for, which, if made, will be used only for the purpose above stated.

The Bank is authorized to obtain from any source any information which it may require to enable or assist it to pass upon this application. If this application is approved, I also authorize the Bank to give credit information to others.

The undersigned knows that you rely and will continue to rely theron until written notice of any change therein is received by you. The undersigned will give you immediate written notice of any material change in the undersigned's financial condition, including any law-suit, begun or threatened, the effect of which may be to materially alter the said condition.

The undersigned will furnish you with such financial statements and data at such times and with such certifications as you may require, without expense to you. You, and your agents and accountants, may at any time inspect the undersigned's books and accounts.

This application shall remain in the property of the Bank, whether approved, not approved, withdrawn, or if the loan is paid.

Signed this   day of   , 19

It is unlawful to deny or stop credit or services or to damage anyone's credit standing because of his or her sex or marital status.

.... (SEAL)
Name of applicant

By ....
Title, if any

By ....
Title, if any

FINAL STAGES

If you're turned down after the analysis period, always ask why and what needs to be changed. If you're approved, it may be conditional, which means the bank may want something else, such as an SBA guarantee. Other conditions may include:

- More equity financing.
- More collateral or personal guarantees.
- A bit more homework.

If you're totally approved, you need to go back to the bank to sign documents and discuss the final arrangements of the loan itself. The following pages contain sample loan and security (collateral) agreements of the kind you may be asked to sign. Read them carefully so you understand what your obligations are before you sign. Your banker may suggest something other than a term loan on a fixed repayment schedule. You may hear words like variable interest rate, balloon payments, chattel mortgages. Be certain to ask questions about things you don't understand and be doubly certain you understand when payments are to be made, how much they are, what interest rate(s) you'll be paying. We use the word "rate(s)" because the bank may propose one loan against inventory, another against real estate, a third against equipment, all with different interest rates and terms. Don't let this dismay you. The bank knows what it's doing; just be sure you know what it's doing, too.

Before you sign anything, here are some key questions to ask the loan officer:

1. Regarding interest—what rate is it? Is it fixed or variable? If it's variable, how much can it vary? When does the interest commence? Can you pay interest only (no principal) for some period?
2. What is the maturity date of the loan? Is the last payment a normal payment or is it higher?
3. What is the price of placement? (*Note:* Some banks charge "points," meaning percentage points. This is a one-time fee. If you borrow $20,000 at two points—2 percent—you will be charged $400).
4. Do you have the right to repay the outstanding balance at any time? Is there a fee to do this?

5. Must you sign a personal guarantee for a business loan? (You will probably be required to do so.)
6. What will you be required to do other than make payments? (*Note:* You may have to maintain certain financial ratios or keep a certain minimum in your checking account, called a compensating balance.)
7. What insurances are you required to have?
8. Can the bank assign the loan to another party?
9. What are you restricted from doing? (Example: paying dividends or high salaries.)
10. What constitutes default? What will happen? What costs will be charged? What is the process with foreclosure?

CONTINUING BANK RELATIONS

If you receive your loan, the worst thing you can do is never cooperate or communicate with your banker again. Bring all your business to that bank—personal checking, savings, certificates of deposit. You're in a total business relationship. Don't shortchange the deal by spreading yourself around. You want someone on your side. Be certain to send quarterly income statements and balance sheets to your banker and plan to take him or her to lunch at least twice a year to share the good news as well as the bad. Your banker doesn't want to hear bad news on the street. If it looks as though you might need additional financing, advise your banker well in advance. Bankers never respond well to what is called "Friday night financing."

In addition, don't switch banks for a couple of percentage points on a loan. You'll only do it once. If you find after a year or so that your bank isn't giving you the service you want, then look for another lending institution.

If things really get rough—sales are much lower than expected or expenses are higher than you planned—your banker will want to see you monthly. You'll have to do a new cash flow projection. If you can't make a loan payment, for goodness sake, call your banker *in advance.* Explain the situation.

BUSINESS LOAN AGREEMENT

TO: THE FIRST NATIONAL BANK OF ANYTOWN.

The undersigned _____

_____ (hereinafter called "Borrower") hereby applies to THE FIRST NATIONAL BANK OF ANYTOWN (hereinafter called "Bank") for a loan (hereinafter called the "loan") to be evidenced by a promissory note which includes the following provisions or such other provisions as to which Borrower and Bank may agree in writing:

Amount of Note: $_____ Date of Note: _____

_____, 19_____

Payable: _____

Borrower, in consideration of Bank making the loan to Borrower, hereby warrants, represents and agrees as follows:

1. The business operations of Borrower are as follows: _____
_____
<small>(Insert type of business, i.e.,</small>

_____ and said business is a _____
<small>machine shop, bakery, etc.)</small>　　　　　　　<small>(Indicate whether sole ownership, partnership, corporation or trust)</small>

2. Borrower will continue said business, will not engage in any other business without permission of Bank, and will use the proceeds of the loan only in connection with said business and for the following purposes:

3. Borrower's balance sheet as at _____

_____ 19_____ and the related statement of income and retained earnings for Borrower's fiscal year ending on such date, both of which have been delivered to Bank, are complete and correct and have been prepared in accordance with generally accepted accounting principles consistently applied throughout the period involved. There are no liabilities of Borrower contingent or otherwise not disclosed in said balance sheet and since the date of such balance sheet there has been no change in the assets, liabilities, financial condition or business of Borrower shown thereon other than changes in the ordinary course of business, the effect of which has not been in the aggregate materially adverse.

4. So long as any amount remains unpaid under the loan:

4.1 Borrower's current business assets will exceed Borrower's current business liabilities, both determined in accordance with generally accepted accounting principles consistent with those applied in preparation of the financial statements referred to in Paragraph 3, by at least _____

_____ Dollars ($_____). If left blank, this provision is not applicable.

4.2 Borrower's current ratio (the relationship of current assets to current liabilities) will be maintained at not less than　　　　. Classification of current assets and current liabilities shall be computed in accordance with generally accepted accounting principles consistently applied.

4.3 Borrower's debt to tangible net worth ratio (the relationship of current and total indebtedness to tangible net worth) shall not exceed
　　　　　　　　For purposes of this Agreement, "tangible net worth" shall mean the aggregate book value of the assets of the Borrower (after deduction therefrom of all applicable reserves and allowances) minus (a) total liabilities, (b) any write-up in the value of assets occurring after the date hereof, and (c) all intangibles including but not limited to goodwill, leasehold improvements, patents, trademarks and the like.

4.4 Borrower's tangible net worth will not be less than $

4.5 Borrower will maintain compensating demand deposit account balances of at least _____ of the outstanding loan balance. If such balances are not maintained, Borrower will be charged a deficiency fee equal in amount to the product of (X) the difference between the required compensating balance and the balance maintained, and (Y) the rate stated in the note of even date herewith for the number of days actually elapsed based on a 360 day year.

4.6 Borrower will furnish to Bank within ninety days after the close of each fiscal year of Borrower, a balance sheet of Borrower as of the close of such year and an income statement and statement of retained earnings for such year for Borrower (or if Borrower is an individual, for Borrower's business) certified by independent public accountants satisfactory to Bank; will furnish to Bank unaudited balance sheet and operating figures for each _____ _____ within thirty days after the end of each of said periods, and such other data as Bank may request; and will at all times permit representatives of Bank to inspect and make extracts from Borrower's books and records.

4.7 Borrower will maintain its books and records relating to its financial affairs at all times in accordance with, and all financial statements provided for herein shall be prepared in accordance with, generally accepted accounting principles consistent with those applied in preparation of the financial statements referred to in Paragraph 3.

4.8 Borrower will not pay any dividends on any class of capital stock or make any other distribution or payment on account of or in redemption of capital stock, or permit any withdrawals from or distributions of the assets of Borrower, or if Borrower is an individual, the business assets of Borrower, except as salary or compensation for services rendered after the date hereof; provided, however, that total payment for services rendered (in cash or otherwise and including dividends, withdrawals, distributions, salary and compensation) in any month to the following may equal but shall not exceed the following amounts:

Name	Monthly Amount

4.9 Borrower will maintain financially sound and reputable insurers, insurance with respect to Borrower's properties and business against such casualties and contingencies and in such types and such amounts as shall be in accordance with sound business practices.

4.10 Without the prior written consent of Bank, Borrower will not:

4.10.1 Incur, assume or permit to exist indebtedness for borrowed money except from the bank.

4.10.2 Sell, factor or borrow on the security of Borrower's accounts receivable with or without recourse, guaranty, endorse (other than for collection or deposit in the regular course of business) or become or remain liable in respect of any indebtedness, obligation or liability of any other person, firm or corporation or permit any such secondary responsibility to exist.

4.10.3 Create or permit to exist any mortgage, pledge or other lien or encumbrance on any of Borrower's property except (i) those arising from attachments or similar proceedings, pending litigation, judgments or taxes or assessments whose validity or amount is currently being contested in good faith by appropriate proceedings and for which adequate reserves have been established and maintained in accordance with generally accepted accounting principles, or taxes and assessments which are not due and delinquent; (ii) liens of carriers, warehousemen, mechanics and materialmen and other like; (iii) pledges or deposits made in connection with workmen's compensation, unemployment or other insurance, old age pensions or other social security benefits, and good faith deposits in connection with tenders, contracts or leases to which Borrower is a party, or deposits to secure, or in lieu of, surety, penalty or appeal bonds, performance bonds and other similar obligations; (iv) encumbrances consisting of easements, rights of way, zoning restrictions, restrictions on the use of real property and similar encumbrances and minor irregularities in title; (v) landlord's liens under leases; and (vi) in favor of Bank.

4.10.4 Purchase or acquire any securities of or make any loans or advances to or investments in any person, firm or corporation except obligations of the United States government or any agency of the United States government or certificates of deposit issued by any one of the fifty largest banks in the United States.

4.10.5 Merge or consolidate or sell or dispose of all or a portion of Borrower's assets other than in the ordinary course of business, or in any way or manner alter Borrower's capital structure, including the sale, transfer or redemption of any shares of the Borrower.

4.10.6 Hire or discharge any officer or retain the services of any independent contractor or professional, except in the ordinary course of business and only where the management of the Borrower is not materially affected or changed.

4.10.7 In any twelve month period spend or become obligated to spend any sum in excess of _____

Dollars ($_____) for the acquisition, construction or installation of properties to be carried in Borrower's books as fixed assets. If left blank, this provision is not applicable.

4.10.8 Incur or assume rental obligations for any current or future period of twelve consecutive months under leases of real or personal property aggregating more than $_____ or

aggregating more than $_____

_____ at any one time outstanding.

5. The loan and any and all other obligations of Borrower to Bank, direct or indirect, absolute or contingent, due or to become due, now existing or hereafter arising (the "Obligations") shall at Bank's option become immediately due and payable without notice or demand at any time after (a) default in the payment or performance of any Obligation; (b) default in the observance by Borrower of any of the terms of this Agreement; (c) death, dissolution, termination of existence, insolvency, business failure, appointment of a receiver of any part of the property of, assignment for the benefit of creditors by, or the commencement of any proceedings under any bankruptcy or insolvency laws by or against Borrower or any party secondarily liable under any of the Obligations.

6. Any deposits or other sums at any time credited by or due from Bank to Borrower and any securities or other property of Borrower in Bank's possession may at all times be held and treated as security for payment of the Obligations. In the event any one or more of the events of default set forth in Paragraph 5 shall have occurred or be continuing, then regardless of the adequacy of any collateral, any deposits or other sums credited by or due from Bank to Borrower may be set off against any and all of the Obligations.

7. Borrower will at all times execute and deliver such further instruments and take such further action as may reasonably be requested by Bank in order to carry out the intent and purposes of this Agreement.

8. No failure or delay on Bank's part in exercising any right hereunder shall operate as a waiver thereof or any other right. No waiver hereunder shall be effective unless in writing and a waiver on any one occasion shall not be a waiver of any right or remedy on any future occasion.

9. In case of a default in the performance of the Obligations, Borrower will pay to Bank such further amount as shall be sufficient to cover the cost and expense of collection including (without limitation) reasonable attorneys' fees and expenses.

10. This Agreement shall be deemed to be a sealed contract under the law of (state) and shall be construed in accordance with such law.

11. Borrower agrees to additional provisions as follows:

_____

_____

_____

_____

_____

_____

_____

_____

_____

_____

_____

IN WITNESS WHEREOF, Borrower has executed and delivered this Loan Agreement this _____

day of _____, 19_____.

_____

_____

SECURITY AGREEMENT

_____
NAME

_____
STREET AND NUMBER   CITY   STATE

(hereinafter called "Debtor"), hereby grants to THE FIRST NATIONAL BANK OF ANYTOWN (hereinafter called "Bank"), to secure the payment of $_____ as provided in the Debtor's note(s) of even date herewith and also to secure the payment and performance of all other obligations of Debtor to Bank, whether direct or indirect, absolute or contingent, due or to become due, now existing or hereafter arising (all of the foregoing, including said notes, being hereinafter called the "Obligations"), a security interest in the following personal property of Debtor and any and all additions, substitutions, accessions and proceeds thereto or thereof (all of the same being hereinafter called the "Collateral"):

Debtor hereby warrants and covenants that—

1. The Collateral will be kept at _____ until such time as written consent to a change of location is obtained from Bank.

2. Except for the security interest granted hereby, Debtor is the owner of the Collateral free from all encumbrances and will defend the same against the claims and demands of all persons. Debtor will not pledge, mortgage or create, or suffer to exist, a security interest in the Collateral in favor of any person other than Bank, and will not sell or transfer the Collateral or any interest therein without the prior written consent of Bank.

3. The Collateral shall remain personal property irrespective of the manner of its attachment to any real estate. If the Collateral is attached to real estate prior to the perfection of the security interest granted hereby, Debtor will on demand of Bank furnish to Bank a disclaimer or disclaimers, signed by all persons having an interest in the real estate, of any interest in the Collateral which is prior to Bank's interest. Debtor will notify Bank in writing of any intended sale, mortgage or conveyancy of any real estate to which the Collateral is at any time attached, and will give written notice of the terms and conditions of this agreement to any prospective purchaser, mortgagee, grantee or other transferee of the real estate or any interest therein.

4. Debtor will immediately notify Bank in writing of any change in address from that shown in this agreement, shall at all reasonable times and from time to time allow Bank, by or through any of its officers, agents, attorneys or accountants, to examine, inspect or make extracts from Debtor's books and records, and shall do, make, execute and deliver all such additional and further acts, things, deeds, assurances and instruments as Bank may require more completely to vest in and assure to Bank its rights hereunder or in any of the Collateral.

5. Debtor will keep the Collateral at all times insured by such insurance as Bank may from time to time require, and in any event and without specific request by Bank, will insure the Collateral against fire, including so-called extended coverage, theft, and, in the case of any motor vehicle, collision, all insurance to be with such insurance companies as Bank shall approve, with loss thereon to be payable to Bank and Debtor as their respective interests may appear. All policies of insurance shall provide for not less than ten days' notice of cancellation or change in form to Bank and, if requested by Bank, shall be delivered to and held by it until all of the Obligations have been fully performed.

6. Debtor will keep the Collateral in good order and repair, and will not use the same in violation of law or any policy of insurance thereon. Bank may inspect the Collateral at any reasonable time, wherever located. Debtor will pay promptly when due all taxes and assessments upon the Collateral or for its use or operation or upon this agreement.

7. In its discretion, Bank may discharge taxes and other encumbrances at any time levied or placed on the Collateral, make repairs, thereof and place and pay for insurance thereon and pay any necessary filing fees. Debtor agrees to reimburse Bank on demand for any and all expenditures so made, and until paid the amount thereof shall be a debt secured by the Collateral. Bank shall have no obligation to Debtor to make any such expenditures nor shall the making thereof relieve Debtor of any default. Bank

may act as attorney for Debtor in making, adjusting and settling claims under any insurance covering the Collateral.

8. Debtor may have possession and use of the Collateral until default. Upon the happening of any of the following events or conditions, namely: (a) default in the payment or performance of any of the Obligations, of any liability or obligation to Bank of any indorser, guarantor or surety of or for any of the Obligations, or of any covenant or liability contained or referred to herein or in any note, instrument, document or agreement evidencing any Obligation; (b) any representation or warranty of Debtor in this agreement or made to Bank by Debtor to induce it to enter into this agreement or to make a loan to Debtor proving false or erroneous in any material respect; (c) loss, theft, material damage, destruction, sale, or encumbrance of or to the Collateral, or the making of any levy thereon or seizure or attachment thereof by legal process; (d) death, dissolution, termination of existence, insolvency, business failure, appointment of a receiver of any part of the property of, assignment for the benefit of creditors by, or the commencement of any proceeding under any bankruptcy or insolvency laws by or against Debtor, or any indorser, guarantor or surety of or for any Obligation; (e) such a change in the management or ownership of Debtor as in the opinion of Bank increases its risk; thereupon, and as long as such default continues, Bank may without notice or demand declare all of the Obligations to be immediately due and payable, and Bank shall then have in any jurisdiction where enforcement hereof is sought, in addition to all other rights and remedies, the rights and remedies of a secured party under the Uniform Commercial Code, including without limitation thereto the right to take immediate possession of the Collateral, and for the purpose Bank may, so far as Debtor can give authority therefor, enter upon any premises on which the Collateral, or any part thereof, may be situated and remove the same therefrom. Debtor will upon demand make the Collateral available to Bank at a place and time designated by Bank which is reasonably convenient to both parties. Bank will give Debtor at least five days' prior written notice of the time and place of any public sale of the Collateral or of the time after which any private sale thereof is to be made. From the proceeds of the sale, Bank shall be entitled to retain (i) all sums secured hereby, (ii) its reasonable expenses of retaking, holding, preparing for sale and selling, and (iii) reasonable legal expenses incurred by it in connection herewith and with such sale. No waiver by Bank or any default shall be effective unless in writing nor operate as a waiver of any other default or of the same default on another occasion.

9. Debtor waives demand, notice, protest, notice of acceptance of this agreement, notice of loans made, credit extended, collateral received or delivered or other action taken in reliance hereon and all other demands and notices of any description. With respect both to the Obligations and the Collateral, Debtor assents to any extension or postponement of the time of payment or any other indulgence, to any substitution, exchange or release of collateral, to the addition or release of any party or person primarily or secondarily liable, to the acceptance of partial payment thereon and the settlement, compromising or adjusting of any thereof, all in such manner and at such time or times as Bank may deem advisable. Bank shall have no duty as to the collection or protection of the Collateral or any income thereon, nor as to the preservation of rights against prior parties, nor as to the preservation of any rights pertaining thereto beyond the safe custody thereof. Bank may exercise its rights with respect to the Collateral without resorting or regard to other collateral or sources of reimbursement for liability. Bank shall not be deemed to have waived any of its rights upon or under the Obligations or the Collateral unless such waiver be in writing and signed by Bank. No delay or omission on the part of Bank in exercising any right shall operate as a waiver of such right or any other right. A waiver on any one occasion shall not be construed as a bar to or waiver of any right on any future occasion. All rights and remedies of Bank on the Obligations or the Collateral, whether evidenced hereby or by any other instrument or papers, shall be cumulative and may be exercised separately or concurrently.

10. This agreement and all rights and obligations hereunder, including matters of construction, validity and performance, shall be governed by the law of (state). This agreement is intended to take effect as a sealed instrument.

IN WITNESS WHEREOF, Debtor has executed _____ original counterparts of this agreement on this _____

day of _____, 19____.

SIGNED AND SEALED
IN THE PRESENCE OF

_____

By_____

_____
    WITNESS

If you get in trouble, you may find your banker ready to help by:

- Restructuring the loan;
- Postponing principal payments;
- Granting more credit;

but only if you explain what's happened and show how you plan to correct the situation. Work with bankers and they'll work with you. They don't want to see you fail in business for several reasons:

1. It's often difficult for a bank to sell collateral and realize their investment from it.
2. A bank has expenses just as you do. If you can't meet your obligations, bank officers have difficulty meeting theirs.
3. If a smaller bank makes *one* business loan at their legal limit and that loan defaults, it alone may erase their entire year's profit.
4. It's a black mark on their record, too.

If you succeed, so do they. It's a nice partnership. Now let's talk briefly about the SBA.

THE SMALL BUSINESS ADMINISTRATION

The U.S. Small Business Administration is an agency of the government chartered specifically to help small business. The SBA treats a franchise just like any other small business, and although the role can change, the SBA has two major purposes:

1. To provide education, information, and direct management assistance (consulting) at little or no cost.
2. To guarantee bank loans made to small business owners.

The SBA does loan some money, but this isn't the rule, and what little lending it does do may end soon.

If you want more information, visit your nearest SBA office. Also read *How to Finance Your Small Business with Government Money: SBA Loans,* by R. Hayes and J. Howell (1980, John Wiley & Sons, New York).

THE SBA'S FINANCIAL ROLE: DIRECT LOANS

We mentioned that the SBA still makes a few *direct* loans but nothing like they used to. This is because, by law, the agency may not make or guarantee a loan if a business can obtain funds on reasonable terms from a bank or other private source. A prospective business owner must seek private financing before applying to the SBA for a loan. You don't go to the SBA until you talk to the bank. If two banks turn you down,* *then* you can talk to the SBA about direct financing. However, the same criteria of personal resources, collateral, and a sound business plan still apply.

Although Congress may change the rules and the financial appropriations, the SBA has had some direct loan money available for:

- Low income and other disadvantaged persons;
- Non-profit sheltered workshops;
- Handicapped persons in business;
- Firms engaged in certain specific energy conservation projects;
- Development companies for projects aiding small businesses;
- Export purposes.

To be eligible for an SBA loan, your business must:

1. Meet certain size limitations (number of employees, sales).
2. Be independently owned and operated, which a franchise is.
3. Be a profit-making venture (except for non-profit sheltered workshops).
4. Not be dominant in its field. (American Motors, with 28,000 employees, once qualified for an SBA loan using this provision.)
5. Not discriminate in its employment.

The SBA will not consider loans on speculative businesses, newspapers, and gambling operations.

As the loan applicant, you must:

1. Be of good character.
2. Show an ability to run a business successfully.

*This holds true in cities with populations greater than 200,000. You need only one refusal in smaller towns.

How You Buy a Franchise

3. Have enough personal capital at stake to withstand losses.
4. Show that the proposed loan is of such sound value or so secured as to reasonably assure payment.

Direct loans are presently limited to $150,000, except that handicapped assistance loans carry a maximum limit of $100,000. Regular business loans have a maximum maturity of 25 years, whereas working capital loans are generally limited to seven years. Interest rates vary with economic conditions.

Collateral must be one or more of the following:

1. A mortgage on land, building(s).
2. A mortgage on chattels. This is a lien against assets like cash registers and vehicles.
3. Assignment of warehouse receipts for marketable merchandise.
4. Guarantees or personal endorsements.
5. In some instances, assignment of current accounts receivable.

The SBA recommends the following steps for those wanting to buy any business:

1. Describe the type of business you plan to buy.
2. Describe your experience and management capabilities.
3. Prepare an estimate of how much you or others have to invest in the business and how much you need to borrow.
4. Prepare a current net worth statement (balance sheet) listing all personal assets and all liabilities.
5. Prepare a detailed projection of earnings for the first year the business operates.
6. List collateral to be offered as security for the loan, indicating your estimate of the present market value of each item.
7. Take the foregoing material to your banker. Ask for a direct bank loan, and if you are declined, ask the bank to consider making the loan under the SBA's Loan Guarantee Plan. If the bank is interested in an SBA guaranteed or participation loan, ask the banker to contact the SBA to discuss your application. In most cases of guaranteed or participation loans, the SBA deals directly with the bank.
8. If a guaranteed or participation loan is not available, write or visit the nearest SBA office. The SBA has 110 field offices which often send loan officers to visit many smaller cities if the need arises. To speed matters, make your financial information available when you first write or visit the SBA.

THE SBA'S FINANCIAL ROLE: GUARANTEED LOANS

The guaranteed loan program is the one you'll most likely use if you go the SBA route. There are advantages and disadvantages to doing so. The advantages are:

- A bank *may* be more willing to make the loan with 70 to 90 percent of it backed by a government agency. If you receive a $50,000 loan which is 90 percent guaranteed by the SBA and you default, the SBA must fork over $45,000 to the bank and then come after you for reimbursement. The bank comes after the remaining $5,000 in a separate action.
- The loan guarantee sometimes permits a bank to do business differently, more flexibly. For example, some states don't allow banks to take second mortgages; with SBA participation, they can.
- The bank *may* be more willing to use a fixed interest rate—say 2½ points over the prime interest rate—rather than a fluctuating one. The fixed rate is generally preferred by business owners because they can plan their interest expense in advance rather than have a constantly changing monthly interest bill.
- If you run into financial difficulty, the SBA may help re-negotiate the loan. As an agency of the U. S. government, the SBA has wide experience with small business, especially its problems. Sometimes a banker and a business owner disagree or even become hostile to one another and the SBA can act as a mediator between them.

Disadvantages are:

- Some banks are reluctant to deal with the SBA; a few refuse outright.
- There's more paperwork, delays, and red tape, although the process has been greatly streamlined in recent years.
- Because of politics, the SBA is often forced to change its methods and policies midstream.
- Some SBA offices aren't as efficient or caring as others.

- Most SBA employees and officers have no direct small business experience; they're career government employees who have never faced business risks.

BANKS, THE SBA, AND YOU

If all works properly, all three parties—the bank, the SBA, and you—benefit:

1. The *bank* gets the guarantee of the U. S. government for a majority of the loan. Bankers like to have two ways to get out of a loan (personal guarantees and business assets, for example) and some look for three. The SBA gives them one way out. Also the bank has an opportunity to make a better profit on the entire transaction. Bankers sell the guaranteed portion of the loan on what is known as the secondary market, get back most of the principal immediately, and collect a processing fee of a couple of percentage points. The buyer of the guaranteed portion, usually a private individual, receives a U.S. government obligation.
2. The SBA fulfills its mission to help small business.
3. *You* get your money.

SUMMARY OF SBA PARTICIPATION

Remember, you don't have to use the SBA. If you can get your bank loan without it, you're better off in the long run because the SBA won't save you either time or money. However, if your banker recommends SBA participation, heed that advice and have patience with the procedure. Even if you're asked to do what you feel are silly things, remember what's at stake—your money and your business.

COMMERCIAL FINANCE COMPANIES

Commercial finance companies are another source of OPM. You can find these institutions in the Yellow Pages under "Loans." Basically, a commercial finance company works with you just like a bank; they want the same documentation and collateral. Some of them are also approved SBA lending institutions. Because finance companies aren't regulated the same way banks are, they can legally take more risk. The default ratio on the amount of outstanding loans is higher, and therefore, so are the interest rates they charge. For this reason and several others, we're not in favor of them. Most aren't very professional in their dealings with small business owners. When you hear advertising like "no limit loans" and "money for any worthwhile purpose," it should make you wonder. The other problem with a finance company is that you're only a borrower to them. If you have a loan from a commercial bank and keep your business and personal accounts there, you're a total customer of that bank. If you run into a financial snag, your banker is going to be more flexible than a finance company.

STATE AND LOCAL DEVELOPMENT AUTHORITIES

Every state and practically every city with a population greater than 10,000 has some kind of development authority. State agencies (usually called economic development departments) won't be of much help to you as a small business owner because they're more interested in larger projects. However, your local authority may be of assistance, especially if you're buying a franchise employing more than one or two people. A book listing all state agencies as well as many other valuable sources is *The Insider's Guide to Small Business Resources* by David E. Gumpert and Jeffry A. Timmons (1982, Doubleday & Co., Garden City, New York).

FARMER'S HOME ADMINSTRATION (FMHA)

There are 1,750 rural counties in the United States that have FmHA offices. Through their Business and Industry Loan Program, the FmHA guarantees bank loans much like the SBA but with a few differences:

1. Priorities are given to truly rural businesses.
2. The major test used by FmHA is whether the business provides real benefits to the community where it's located. These benefits include more jobs and/or attracting money from outside the community—tourism, for example.

If you plan to open a franchise in a rural area, check your phone book listing under U.S. Government—Agriculture Department. Because FmHA's ground rules change from time to time, it's a good idea to call before visiting them.

CUSTOMERS

If your franchise is perceived as a good business by your potential customers, they might want to invest. Another method of financing is to have customers pay in advance; however, this must be handled very carefully or you may lose them as customers completely. Check with the franchisor on this.

SUPPLIERS

Again, they may want to invest, but a more common route is the use of trade credit. You may find some suppliers willing to extend credit for 30 days and even longer, but it's more likely you'll have to pay cash for your first orders. If you don't ask, you'll never know.

EMPLOYEES

If you're going to sell stock to employees, be sure to check with your lawyer first. You may unwittingly create an ESOP—Employee Stock Option Plan—and that has legal ramifications. If you simply plan to borrow money from them, the loan is a standard business loan.

AN INTERESTING ALTERNATIVE

It's been said that we're a nation of innovators and that's true in nearly every field you can think of, including financing. When traditional methods of raising money for very young companies with high growth potential failed to provide enough risk capital, we invented venture capital. When banks got clobbered in the 1970s, caught with long-term, fixed interest rate loans at 5 to 9 percent, and had to pay up to 15 percent for new certificates of deposit, they switched to variable interest loans.

With franchisors providing little financing, a new company—Franchise Finance Corporation of America (FFCA)*—was born in 1980 to meet that need. Now FFCA is well on its way to raising a total of one *billion* dollars. Before you get too excited, there are some major restrictions in the FFCA program. In the first place, FFCA only works with franchisees who want a fast-food restaurant and then the list they consider is limited—Arby's, Taco Bell, Long John Silver's, Kentucky Fried Chicken, Church's Fried Chicken, Jack in the Box, Grandy's Country Cookin', Bojangles, Rax Restaurants, Sisters Chicken & Biscuits, and Del Taco are representative. Secondly, the financing is only for land, building and equipment, not for the franchise fee, supplies, and working capital.

What FFCA does, with the help of an underwriter, is to raise money through public offerings from private and institutional sources. FFCA then buys the land, building, and equipment and leases them back to you. You rent the land and building (real estate), paying 14.5 percent per year of the cost of the real estate, or 6 percent of your gross sales, whichever is greater. The lease typically runs 20 years with renewal options plus an option for you to buy the real estate at fair market value (FMV) any time after the 10th year. The annual equipment lease amounts to 14.5 percent of its cost and runs for 8 years. No principal payments are included in the lease payments, but you can buy the equipment at the end of the 8th year for about 10 percent of its initial cost.

The advantages of this approach are many—lower initial cash requirement on the part of the franchisee, fixed rate financing, fixed terms of the lease, buyback capability, better tax advantage.

Even though you may not qualify for FFCA financing, it's a unique approach and other firms may begin considering smaller franchises and in fields other than fast-food. Ask your franchisor.

MISCELLANEOUS SOURCES

Some other interesting sources can be found if you look around. Small foundations exist to give financial aid to people in business and many of

*3443 North Central Avenue, Phoenix, AZ 85012

these are restricted to people of a particular ethnic group, geographic location, or even place of birth. Take the time to ask around. Also contact the professional trade association(s) that serves your type of business.

Other sources to consider are:

- Venture capitalists*
- Local stock investment clubs
- Credit unions
- Savings and loan associations
- College endowment funds
- Charitable trusts

*For a more lengthy description of venture capital, see Brian R. Smith's *Raising Seed Money For Your Own Business* (1984, Lewis Publishing Company/The Stephen Greene Press).

- Tax-exempt foundations
- Large employers in your town.

Ultimately, of course, the most important source of financing for your business is the profit it produces.

SUMMARY

By now you should be ready to begin your life as a franchisee and independent business owner. Are we finally going to let you sign that agreement and make out that check? Not quite yet. There are still a few considerations which we'll discuss in the next (and final) chapter.

CHAPTER 12

Getting Under Way

BEFORE YOU (FINALLY) SIGN THE AGREEMENT

In this last chapter in our journey together, let's review where we've been and then examine some last-minute details. Early in the book we provided an overview of franchising and followed that with some self-evaluation procedures and ways to determine possible franchise opportunities. Then we discussed initial and direct contacts with potential franchisors, the franchisor's preliminary material and the FTC disclosure material and the franchise agreement. Next we studied how to evaluate any financial data received from the franchisor. Finally we examined the full and comparative analysis of any franchises you're considering and ways to secure any outside financing if necessary.

We've deliberately held you back from signing the agreement and sending your deposit or franchise fee because we want you to work through the proper steps in advance. Once you sign, it's too late to make any changes. At this point you're probably at one of three places:

1. You've decided franchising isn't the route for you. If you're still interested in having your own business, you'll probably buy an existing one or start one of your own.
2. You're a bit unsure of franchising and will delay any action for now.

3. You've picked your franchise and are ready to get under way.

Let's assume you're in the third category; you've done your homework and have found what you think is the right franchise for you. Let's also assume the franchising company still has locations or a location in the town where you want to start your business. If you were buying a house or an existing business, the obvious first step would be to make an offer, but the FTC ruling, in effect, stops you from offering the franchisor less than the asking price for the franchise. Even if the franchisor is willing to sell it to you for less because you convinced them you'll be the best franchisee they ever had, they (and you) still have a problem. If the franchisor sells you the franchise for less than the going rate, they must now put that "reduced price" in their disclosure documentation. When the next prospect sees that, you can be sure he or she will want the same price break you got. To be sure, franchisors don't have to print a new disclosure every time they sell a franchise or bend a rule, but it had better be in the next one they do print. Furthermore, if the franchisor tells you they don't charge less than the current franchise fee, but have in the past, they're probably also in violation of The Rule. However, in our experience, franchisors just don't lower the franchise price; the risks they run in doing so make it more trouble than it's worth.

Some franchisors may provide some financing terms even if the FTC disclosure states the company doesn't. As we suggested earlier, it's important to ask if the company will accept terms on the franchise fee. It doesn't hurt to ask, and it can definitely benefit you because the more cash you have available, the more chance you have to build a successful business. No franchisor wants to take terms on the franchise fee, but if they like you, want a unit in your area, and haven't had many takers, they may be willing to accept them.

Your only real point of negotiation in the purchase of your franchise is the geographical area or territory. This has little value if you live in an isolated mid-sized city and the franchisor intends to put a unit there whether you're the owner or someone else is. However, in many cases you can argue the point that, before you sign the agreement, you feel you need a much larger area than they're offering. Bear in mind that each franchisor handles territory a little differently. Rather than open up a territory to all comers, some may simply limit the number of offices or units they place in an area. For example the franchisor may tell you (and put it in writing) that there will not be more than a certain number of units or franchises in your city. Obviously this limits the number of locations available, but there can be one condition you should watch for. If the franchisor limits the number of units, make sure you see it is so worded that there will only be a certain number of units in the area *for a certain period of time*. If your agreement is for five years, and renewable every five years thereafter, the limiting number of units may hold only for the first five years. In other cases the agreement may state that there will be no other units for a shorter period of time. Make sure you are aware of any time period and if there is one, that you understand it. If there's no time period defined, don't make the mistake of believing that means that number is fixed forever. The most anything in that contract is guaranteed for is the duration of the contract unless stated, in writing, otherwise.

The point is that many franchisors will make concessions to get you on board as a franchisee.

However, although they may want you as a person, they also want your franchise fee and their unit in your area. Therefore, they may be quite willing to make short-term concessions that soon expire and aren't renewed once you're within the system. To a franchisor, getting a franchise up and running is like adding another notch to their gun. Franchising is a numbers business; the more franchisees, the more royalty income and the bigger the company gets. Franchisors tend to talk number of units, as opposed to number of dollars they're making. So when you buy a franchise, you're seen as adding to the total number of units the franchising company can boast about. However, franchising companies aren't the only ones who like to brag; franchisees themselves like to see the number of units increase. Not only does it make them feel like they belong to a fast-growing company; it also helps justify their own decision to become part of it.

Besides money and territory, there's another part of the agreement you may want to address before you affix your signature thereto—to use the lawyer's phraseology. Earlier we talked about a Curry Copy Center franchisee who added a clause to his contract making that agreement null and void if the franchisor failed. Another individual had a franchisor strike a clause that prevented her from operating any other business because she already owned a small mail-order operation. A third individual, concerned about what he perceived as a possible lack of franchisor support, made the franchisor agree in writing to provide an operational visit once a month. When the franchisor failed to meet this commitment, the franchisee refused to pay royalties. In this case, a simple provision provided the franchisee with a way out when the franchisor didn't comply with the terms.

Again, it never hurts to ask about making possible changes. Usually you'll be dealing with a franchise salesperson who probably works on some form of commission arrangement. Therefore, they may be willing to negotiate an area of the agreement that concerns you, if for no other reason than to make the sale and earn their money.

Finally, let's take one last look at the FTC disclosure material and the franchise agreement. The disclosure material is your primary source of information about the franchisor and how they conduct their business. The franchise agreement is not only a legal document that both sides must honor, but just as importantly it's an operating agreement; it tells how you and the franchisor are going to work together. Before you sign it, make sure you understand what the franchisor expects of you. Look at the time periods you have to file royalties and/or service fees; look at the frequency and number of reports you must file. If you don't understand, get clarification. For example, new or relatively new franchise companies can be lax in initially enforcing the reporting requirements in the franchise agreement, but then one day they get a new accountant or consultant who decides the company should get all those reports you didn't file. If the number of or the frequency of reports seems high, see if they'll eliminate some, or change the time periods. For example, if your business is seasonal, you may feel spending time writing reports during your busiest period is counterproductive. However, because the franchisor may be anxious to get data from peak times as soon as possible to plan any changes or expansions, they may insist on it. If you feel either the frequency or the timing of the reports will be detrimental to your successful operation of the business, state your reasons clearly. If they agree, make sure they verify this in writing.

If the franchisor makes these changes, aren't they in violation of the FTC requirements? To be sure, the franchising company may tell you that they can't negotiate the agreement because of the Federal Trade Commission requirement. They may also tell you, and correctly so, that by granting any major change to you they would have to disclose these changes to any new prospects they talk to. They may tell you you can take the agreement to 27 attorneys and read it over 52 times yourself, but the agreement is still not negotiable. However, in the end most franchising companies will amend or amplify any area of the contract that is either ambiguous or needs further clarification. After all, they are in business to sell franchises, not discourage potential buyers.

It's sad but true that the FTC is a mixed blessing. While they require full disclosure to a prospective franchisee, they have completely eliminated practically all negotiating power a prospective franchisee may have. The FTC requirements do, in fact, create a price-fixing mechanism in which a prospect can't negotiate the price or terms or any other areas of the contract with the franchisor. In fairness to the franchisor, their reluctance to do any negotiating or discounting of the price or offer terms on the franchise fee is often based on their awareness they would have to disclose any changes to all past, present, and future franchisees. Although they may recognize the changes you request are very sound in your particular case, they'd rather risk losing a good franchisee now and then than spend the time and money to revamp their entire system to accommodate those changes. Plus, it is easier to take a stand against negotiation of the agreement than to open the "floodgates" to negotiate once the franchisor agrees to capitulate on one point. The whole agreement is now open for negotiation.

Look for any "don't-know-how-they-got-in-there" provisions of the agreement, which some franchise experts call "throwaways." These are clauses or provisions that really don't make a lot of sense or are so outrageous they shouldn't be in the agreement at all. Most franchisors are willing to eliminate them if called upon to do so. Our favorite is one that even most attorneys don't catch. It goes something like this:

> If franchisor feels that franchisee needs additional help or assistance, then franchisor agrees to furnish such assistance at sole expense of the franchisee.

In other words, if the franchisor decides you need help, they'll supply it, but guess who's going to pay for it.

The agreement you're considering may contain such provisions so read it carefully. Unfortunately, by asking the franchisor to eliminate even such a ridiculous provision may mean they'll fight you on any other change you want, using the argument they already yielded to your desires once. Realizing this as a possibility, you may want to rank any desired changes beforehand as "must have," "would like to have," or "can live without" before you enter negotiations. That way you won't wind up making a big fuss and winning some minor point, only to have to yield on something you perceive as crucial to your success.

Before signing the franchise agreement, get all of your questions answered to your satisfaction. Then, and this is very important, get the final resolution or any changes different from the original agreement *in writing*. The executives of your franchising company may be upright and honest people, but they may also be gone tomorrow. The new people may not, and most likely won't, honor any verbal commitments made by any predecessor no matter how high in the executive ranks they may have been. Keep a file of all correspondence between you and the franchisor. For example, if you send them a letter describing your understanding of, or your position on a particular issue, keep a copy of that letter. A good franchisor is doing the same thing. They want a record of everything they've done to and for the franchisee in case the relationship gets to the point where evidence is needed. You should keep a file for the same reason. You certainly don't want to enter a relationship thinking you may have to prove your point, but you never know. Some franchisors say the franchisor/franchisee relationship is like a marriage. In some respects that's true, but it's also a business relationship; files should be maintained of the ongoing business relationship between franchisor and franchisee, just like in any other business situation. This not only protects you, it's sound business practice. The last thing you need as a business owner is to waste valuable time trying to remember what the franchisor told you three weeks ago about a shipment of supplies due today. Nor do you want to be caught like a dummy, stammering on the phone because you can't remember the exact facts and figures the franchisor is referring to in the letter you sent them last week. There's no reason to try to carry all that information around in your head; on the other hand, you should have some sort of filing system that enables you to put your hands on it quickly if necessary.

Once you're certain you understand all the disclosure material, have had any parts of the agreement changed if necessary, and have those changes verified in writing, you're ready to sign. Whatever you do, don't sign something you don't understand because "that'll be explained during your training." Maybe it will, maybe it won't, or maybe it will be too late. If any information is withheld pending your signature, take that as a strong warning you ought to have serious doubts about signing at all.

SELECT YOUR LOCATION

We strongly recommend you try to select your location prior to your training period because some franchises are more dependent on location than others. Food and other retail outlets are very location dependent, much more so than service franchises. However, make sure your site has been approved by the franchisor if that's in your agreement, and even if it's not. There's no sense having the franchisor tell you at some point that you either violated the agreement or chose a lousy location. Take your time and get the best possible location you can find. It's our experience that in their desire to save money and get started quickly, too many franchisees either select inadequate space or a lousy location. We can't prove it, but it seems that most successful franchisees have the best possible location and facilities.

We also recommend you select your location before you attend your training program because the training is geared toward operating your business rather than locating it. Most likely you'll leave the training program full of enthusiasm for your new business and ready to begin. To begin looking for a location at that time creates several problems:

1. In your enthusiasm to get started, you may be tempted to lease the first place you find available.
2. If you spend time selecting a location, you may forget some of what you learned about operating that business during your training.
3. The longer the time between when you leave your training and open your business, the more likely that critical enthusiasm and confidence gained from the training will wane.
4. The longer the time between training and opening your doors, the longer the period when you have money going out and none coming in.

Therefore, take the time before your training to select your site and get the franchisor's approval. That way the necessary papers can be drawn up during your training and the franchisor's subsequent lease approval becomes a mere formality. This frees you to immerse yourself immediately into activities directly related to getting your business up and running when your training is complete.

TRAINING PROGRAMS

You'll find that most franchise training programs are excellent and their instructors competent. Many have had actual field experience and usually are both knowledgeable and concerned. Responsible franchisors put their best people in their training department, so pay attention and take notes. Don't stay out late at night, don't party, and be prepared to work hard. Remember: many franchise agreements contain a provision that says that if you don't pass the training course, the franchisor reserves the right to cancel the whole thing and refund the franchise fee or at least a good portion of it. This isn't just a convenient loophole that allows them to dump you; it also protects you, too. For example, if after a few days of the franchise training program you find yourself in over your head, or realize that the business you are about to enter isn't for you, tell the franchisor. Too many people tell themselves their doubts will go away or at least lessen: they don't! Get out now and you'll probably get a good portion of your money back; wait and you could lose everything. A good franchisor doesn't want to spend a lot of time and money training a franchisee only to have him or her fail, any more than you want to waste your time and money operating a business you don't enjoy. If you have a problem or a question, let it out. It's crucial you leave the training with the enthusiasm and self-confidence necessary to sustain you through your preparations and first months of business.

HOW LONG WILL IT TAKE?

How long the process of becoming a franchised business owner takes depends on you and the franchisor. Times vary considerably from a few weeks to nearly a year. However, most franchisors will provide some form of timetable similar to this:

Day	Activity
Preliminary	Application received and reviewed. Visit to franchisor's headquarters.
1	Franchisee approved; letter of intent signed.

Day	Activity
25	Business plan developed. Financing secured. Site selected.
100	Franchise agreement signed.
115	Franchise training class.
160	Lease approved.
220	Any necessary plans for site changes drawn. Inventory, equipment, supplies ordered.
280	Grand opening.

This nine-month period is what this particular franchisor considers their maximum start-up time. However, they also note in their material that this can be accomplished in as little as three months. Because this interval represents a period when you will have no income coming in from your business, you want to be sure you know how the franchisor came up with these figures and how variable they are.

Although circumstances may prevent you from timing the events as we recommend, try to keep the interval between training and opening your business as short as possible. Take any extra time to develop a sound business plan, line up your financing and choose your business location *before* your training. Nine times out of ten, the problems franchisees get into later result from faulty preparations in these areas. To have to go back and do the job right later not only makes the start-up process take much longer, it costs you money and takes a lot of the fun out of what should be an exciting event.

THE FINAL STEPS

Now your training is complete and you're ready for business. Whether you have a grand opening will largely depend on your type of business and/or the franchisor's operating plan. In either event, you're now officially open for business!

The first 90 days of operation are critical to your success; therefore, you want as much operational support as possible from your franchisor. During this period you should be in constant touch with the person responsible for your geographical area. If no one has been assigned to your business, find a contact person at the corporate headquarters you can talk to who can provide you with the necessary answers to your questions or problems. Don't be afraid to ask as many questions as is necessary to get you started on the right foot. Ed Telling, a VR Business Brokerage franchisee in Syracuse, New York, called the corporate offices at least once a week when he first started out. Ed feels that if he hadn't done this, he wouldn't have been as successful as he is now. Unfortunately, some franchisees wait 90 days, then call their franchisor, panic-stricken, to tell them they're having problems. Don't wait; if you have a question or problem, get it answered now. If you need additional operational support, call and keep calling again until you get it.

Unfortunately, some franchisors are only interested in selling the franchise, and either don't have the necessary support staff or have one that is already overburdened with start-up franchisees just like you. Other franchisors simply aren't qualified to work with new franchisees. If you run into either of these situations, get in touch with someone at the corporate office, including the president of the company if necessary. In the excitement and confusion of these early days, too many franchisees forget the fact that the franchisor *owes* them sufficient start-up assistance and help to see that their business gets started on the right foot. That's what you *paid* them for. If your telephone calls aren't returned or are just plain ignored, send a telegram; do something to get their attention. The old adage, "The squeaking wheel gets the oil" is very true in franchising. Don't get stalled or put off; insist on an immediate response to your problems.

In closing, remember that the relationship between you and the franchisor isn't, nor should it be one of two adversaries battling to see who "wins." Although it may appear that in some cases we've been a bit harsh on franchisors, our intent is to inform you, not to incriminate them. Over 90 percent of the more than 2,000 franchisors in the United States are reputable, honest companies that realize the true value of the win-win situation; if their franchisees succeed, so do they. On the other hand, we can't agree with

the many books and articles that make franchising sound like a sure thing, an infallible way to be successful in your own business. If there is such a sure thing, we've never seen it. Still, the franchise route is less fraught with risk than buying a going concern, certainly risk-wise, and head and shoulders above starting a business of your own.

That franchising fills a real need is evidenced by its growth not only in the United States and Canada, but in other countries as well. Will we reach a stage, as some observers speculate, where nearly every business is a franchise? We doubt it, because there will always be those small business owners who want total autonomy and independence. They simply don't want someone telling them how to run their business, nor do they like the idea of paying to use someone else's name, products, and methods.

If the person who starts up his or her own business represents the most independent approach to employment and the employed worker the most dependent, franchising can fulfill the needs of those who find either extreme uncomfortable. As such, it is possible that it has more to offer more of the working population than these two more commonly recognized forms of employment.

So when you plunk down that franchising fee, what are you really buying—A nationally recognized name? Pre-selected equipment? Inventory that gets converted into a saleable product? True, you are buying all these things; but what you're really buying is a proven method of doing business that agrees with your personal philosophy— whether that business is a chicken-and-dumplings restaurant, a tax service, or an auto tune-up garage. You hope that franchise concept came into being because someone or a group of some- ones were able to run their business so successfully they could refine their procedures in such a way they could (1) teach it to others, and (2) insure that anyone with their training and the right mixture of money, brains, and desire could also succeed in that business whether it's in Saskatoon, Saskatchewan or Kissemee, Florida.

Will franchising continue to grow in the future? We believe it will, but probably not at the rapid rate of the 1960s and 1970s. Many people are discovering the working-for-someone-else route doesn't fulfill all their personal goals and desires.

The security that comes from working 40 years or more for someone else, culminating in a gold watch and a fixed pension, doesn't have the appeal it once had. For these people, franchising offers, and will continue to offer, one alternative to corporate servitude. Other folks who would have routinely started up their own businesses in the past are now also considering franchised alternatives. For example, the high costs of their education and those associated with opening their own offices have led many young professionals (accountants, lawyers, physicians, dentists, veterinarians, optometrists) to explore the franchise route. Whether or not this trend continues depends on the individual personalities of those involved. Those who get into a franchise because they can't go into business for themselves or don't want to work for someone else, don't have nearly the chance of succeeding as those who select the franchise route because they believe it's the best route for them.

But how can you be sure franchising is the best route for you? Do your homework: collect and evaluate your personal data and that from the franchisor(s), seek advice from your lawyer, banker, accountant, other franchisees, or business consultants to fill in any gaps. Then, when you're convinced you have the information you need, take it to the only expert who can tell you whether franchising is or isn't right for you: you.

By recognizing this is a choice that you—not the franchisor, your lawyer, accountant, banker, or mother-in-law—willingly make and accept full responsibility for, you take the most difficult but also the most rewarding step toward becoming a successful business owner.